Ellen White & the Trinity

By
Pastor Jan Voerman

World rights reserved. This book or any portion thereof may not be copied or reproduced in any form or manner whatever, except as provided by law, without the written permission of the publisher, except by a reviewer who may quote brief passages in a review.

The author assumes full responsibility for the accuracy of all facts and quotations as cited in this book. The opinions expressed in this book are the author's personal views and interpretations, and do not necessarily reflect those of the publisher.

This book is provided with the understanding that the publisher is not engaged in giving spiritual, legal, medical, or other professional advice. If authoritative advice is needed, the reader should seek the counsel of a competent professional.

Copyright © 2014 TEACH Services, Inc.
ISBN-13: 978-1-47960-252-0 (Paperback)
ISBN-13: 978-1-47960-253-7 (ePub)
ISBN-13: 978-1-47960-254-4 (Mobi)
Library of Congress Control Number: 2013952502

Published by

www.TEACHServices.com • (800) 367-1844

All scripture quotations, unless otherwise indicated, are taken from the King James Version. Public domain.

Scripture quotations marked (ASV) are taken from the American Standard Version. Public domain.

Scripture quotations marked (Goodspeed) are taken from *The Complete Bible: An American Translation* by Edgar Goodspeed, translator. Published by the University of Chicago Press, October 1939.

Scripture quotations marked (NEB) are taken from The New English Bible. Copyright ©1961, 1970. Used by permission of Oxford University Press and Cambridge University Press. All rights reserved worldwide.

Scripture quotations marked (Phillips) are taken from *The New Testament in Modern English* by J. B. Phillips, 1962 edition, published by HarperCollins.

Scripture quotations marked (Rotherham) are taken from the Rotherham's Emphasized Bible, 1902. Public domain.

Scripture quotations marked (RSV) are taken from the Revised Standard Version of the Bible, copyright 1952 [2nd edition, 1971] by the Division of Christian Education of the National Council of the Churches of Christ in the United States of America. Used by permission. All rights reserved.

Other books in English written by Jan Voerman: *The Hidden Agenda*; *Secret Messages in the Church*; and *The Ordination of Women*.

Jan Voerman also writes books in Dutch, German, Spanish and Danish.

Contents

Introduction 7

Chapter 1. Was Ellen White Really a Semi-Arian?............. 9

Chapter 2. Ellen White and the Holy Spirit 43

Chapter 3. Did Ellen White Reverse Her Belief?............... 55

Chapter 4. Ellen White's Description of God 73

Chapter 5. Ellen White, a Trinitarian................................... 81

Chapter 6. Christ's Subjection to the Father..................... 101

Chapter 7. Christ, the Source of Wisdom 107

Bibliography 113

Introduction

In some parts of the world, questions have arisen in Adventist circles about the Trinity and Ellen White's role in the Church's understanding of the nature of God. Were the early pioneers of our church, including Ellen White, harmoniously united on the nature of the Father, Son, and Holy Spirit? Did Ellen White go along with mistaken notions in the name of unity? Are her repeated appeals to the original platform of eternal truth an indictment against the church for having stepped off the platform since that time? Do her statements correct mistaken concepts held by some Adventist pioneers?

Some people think that Ellen White, in her early ministry, did not believe in the Trinity. They call attention to statements she made, which they believe reflect aspects of semi-Arianism. The circulation of these statements with their appraisal of them often causes commotion and brings confusion to many Adventist believers. It also calls Ellen White's credibility, as an expounder of sound doctrine, into question and raises doubts about whether we should consider her early statements as being completely reliable on all points or whether we would do better to read only her later writings, when she was, as is argued, more mature in her thinking.

Is it possible for a true prophet, called by God, to write and proclaim a deficient message for a period of time? If it is, then how can we distinguish a true prophet from a false one, when both can come up with unsound messages? This question understandably puzzles many sincere believers. What is the truth of the matter? Did Ellen White, in her early ministry, write deficient messages? How can we know? If we study the subject with a prayerful attitude and an honest and open mind, we can know.

As we study about the Godhead, we must recognize that we are finite and sinful human beings. Ellen White wrote: "We must not measure God or His truth by our finite understanding, or by our preconceived opinions" (*Review and Herald*, Oct. 8, 1889). Human reasoning and logic are inadequate to define God. Angels veil their faces before God's presence. With what awe and reverence should we, as fallen sinful beings, approach the holy God and a study of His nature! May God's blessing be with us as we contemplate with consecrated heart the things that God has been pleased to reveal to us.

Chapter 1

WAS ELLEN WHITE REALLY A SEMI-ARIAN?[1]

To answer the question posed by the title of this chapter, it will be well to look first at the three basic positions regarding the nature of God, Christ and the Holy Spirit. These basic positions are Trinitarianism, Arianism, and Semi-Arianism.

TRINITARIANISM is the orthodox belief that there is only one living, true God, or "Godhead," in a unity of three eternal divine Persons: the Father, the Son, and the Holy Spirit. These are of one substance, power, authority, and glory. True orthodox Trinitarian dogma insists on three different *hupostases* (or *ousia*) in one Being—a Tri-Unity.

ARIANISM is named after Arius, who was a presbyter of Alexandria in the fourth century, who ostensibly denied

---

1. For a paper that depicts Ellen White as gradually shifting from semi-Arianism to Trinitarianism, see "Arianism, Adventism and Methodism: The Healing of Trinitarian Teaching and Soteriology," available at www.sdanet.org/atissue/trinity/TrinityWhidden.htm (accessed 9/23/2013).

that Christ was of the same substance as the Father and believed that the Son was created, though He pre-existed before the creation of the world.[2] The Nicaean Council condemned this belief in AD 325.

SEMI-ARIANISM is a compromise between the orthodox and Arian belief on Christ's nature. It teaches that, though Christ was not created, He does not have the same nature as God. Rather, He is subordinate to the Father and not of one substance with Him. While Arian belief alleges that Christ was of a different nature and substance than the Father, semi-Arian belief holds that Christ is begotten of the Father and, therefore, has the exact same nature by inheritance.

As we now consider the question of whether Ellen White was semi-Arian in her belief about Christ, we need to look at the key quotations and arguments that are presented as evidence for that assertion and determine whether the arguments stand up to scrutiny.

---

2. The actual beliefs of Arius are uncertain as there are no extant records of his writings. His opponents destroyed all of his writings and have left only prejudiced accounts of his teaching. In *Truth Triumphant* (1944), page 142, B. G. Wilkinson quotes Dutch theologian Philipp van Limborch (1633–1712) as doubting that Arius ever believed that Christ was created rather than being begotten of the Father in eternity. Limborch wrote: "The *Arian* Controversy, that made such Havock in the Christian Church, was, if I may be allowed to speak it without Offence, in the Beginning only, about Words; though probably, some of *Arius* his Party went farther afterwards than *Arius* himself did at first. *Arius*, as hath been shewn, expressly allowed the Son to be *before all Times and Ages, perfect God, unchangeable*, and begotten after the most perfect Likeness of the unbegotten Father" (*The History of the Inquisition*, vol. 1, p. 95, originally published in Latin in 1692 as *Historia Inquisitionis*).

Quotation Number 1

The Father's Person

Those who believe that Ellen White held semi-Arian views early in her ministry do so based on statements she made to inform and encourage Adventist believers. Here is the first of these:

> "I have often seen the lovely Jesus, that He is a *person*. I asked Him if His Father was a person and had a form like Himself. Said Jesus, 'I am in the express *image* of My Father's *person*.'" (*Early Writings*, p. 77; cf. Heb. 1:3)

Some interpret this description as being semi-Arian because it indicates that the Father and the Son have separate bodies with parts. They therefore conclude that Ellen White was presenting a semi-Arian view of the Father and the Son. Yet, can we rightly assert that Ellen White was presenting her own view when she tells us that she was describing what she saw and heard in vision? This would certainly be unfair and unwarranted. After all, who was it that gave Ellen White her visions? If this vision was given her by God, which we believe to be true, and we brand this vision as being semi-Arian, then we make God responsible for giving Mrs. White a semi-Arian depiction.

Note further that Ellen White does not at all say here that the Father and the Son are completely separate or that they do not share the same nature and substance. There is not a word about that in this statement. To label Ellen White as being a semi-Arian on the basis of this statement, is inconsistent and unsound. To properly interpret a statement requires taking it in its context.

The statement in *Early Writings* was taken from *Spiritual Gifts,* vol. 2, page 74. There, the preceding paragraphs give the reason that Ellen White called attention to Jesus' personhood and why she asked Jesus whether His Father was also a person. Ellen White explains: "Different errors were affecting the Advent people. The spiritual view of Christ's coming, that great deception of Satan, was ensnaring many, and we were often obliged, through a sense of duty, to bear a strong testimony against it" (*Spiritual Gifts,* vol. 2, p. 72). No wonder Ellen White stressed the personhood of the Father and Son. Many were ensnared by the belief that Christ's coming was spiritual and not actual and personal.

These ensnared ones were also spiritualizing away the import of Ellen White's visions. She says: "I knew their only object was to mangle the visions, spiritualize away their literal meaning, and throw a satanic influence upon me, and call it the power of God" (*Spiritual Gifts,* vol. 2, p. 73). This spiritualizing influence was a real threat to Ellen White and the Advent people. Ellen White explains:

> Those were troublesome times. If we had not stood stiffly then, we should have made shipwreck of our faith.... Those who believed in the spiritual coming of Christ, were so insinuating, like the serpent in the garden, to suit their purpose they would profess such a mild, meek spirit, that we had to be on our guard, strengthened on every side with scripture testimony concerning the literal, personal appearing of our Saviour. (*Spiritual Gifts*, vol. 2, p. 74)

Next comes Ellen White's statement, "I have often seen the lovely Jesus, that he is a *person* ..." The concern over personhood was that, if Jesus were not a person, He would not be expected to come back to earth as a person. His coming could then be pictured in a spiritual way, as the ensnared believers ardently insisted. With the context of the statement as background, Ellen White's vision about the personhood of Christ and the Father makes perfect sense. If we ignore the context and maintain that this statement reflects some kind of semi-Arianism, then we miss the statement's purpose.

In Ellen White's day, different views about God circulated, and spiritualistic views took a rather prominent place. On the same page as the statement on Jesus' personhood, Ellen White wrote: "I have frequently been falsely charged with teaching views peculiar to Spiritualism." Following the statement about the Father and Son's personhood, she added: "I have often seen that the spiritual view took away all the glory of heaven, and that in many minds the throne of David and the lovely person of Jesus have been burned up in the fire of Spiritualism" (*Early Writings*, p. 77).

In a testimony written in November 1905, Ellen White listed frequently used spiritualistic representations of God that she considered misleading:

> "The Father is as the light invisible; the Son is as the light embodied; the Spirit is the light shed abroad." "The Father is like the dew, invisible vapor; the Son is like the dew gathered in beauteous form; the Spirit is like the dew fallen to the seat of life." Another representation: "The Father is like the invisible vapor; the Son is like the leaden cloud; the Spirit is rain fallen and working in refreshing power." All these spiritualistic representations are simply nothingness. They are imperfect, untrue. (*Special Testimonies*, Series B, No. 7, p. 62)

Although these "spiritual views" were meant to illustrate the Trinity, it is clear that Ellen White believed that they leave people open to the spiritualistic teaching that God is not real and that Christ's coming is not literal, but only spiritual.[3] The vision in *Early Writings*, page 77, which God gave Ellen White, had nothing to do with semi-Arianism; it was a response to false spiritual views. Jesus' response to Mrs. White's question specifically contradicts the view that the Father and the Son are mystically like dew or vapor, for they are both real persons. Ellen White explained this as she continued in the statement in *Special Testimonies*:

> The Father can not be described by the things of earth. The Father is all the fulness of the Godhead bodily, and is invisible to mortal sight. The Son is all the fullness of the Godhead manifested. The Word of God declares Him to be "the express image of His person." (*Special Testimonies*, Series B, No. 7, p. 62)

Ellen White wrote this in 1905. Does this contradict her statement in *Early Writings?* Like the statement in *Early Writings*, this statement does not assert that the Father and the Son are completely separate or uniquely different in nature and substance. Furthermore, her later statement in *Patriarchs and Prophets* (1890) does not depict the Father and the Son as occupying separate thrones

---

3. Ellen White likely took these representations from *The Higher Christian Life*, pages 102–104, by Trinitarian author William E. Boardman. (This book is listed in Ellen White's library.) Boardman concluded: "These likenings are all imperfect. They rather hide than illustrate the tri-personality of the one God, for they are not persons but things, poor and earthly at best, to represent the living personalities of the living God. So much they may do, however, as to illustrate the official relations of each to the others, and of each and all to us. And more. They may also illustrate the truth that all the fulness of Him who filleth all in all, dwells in each person of the Triune God." Vapor, cloud, and rain, as the three phases of water, is a favorite Trinitarian illustration.

before Jesus' *mission* to earth. On the contrary, it portrays them as sharing the *same* throne, encircled by the *same* glory (*Patriarchs and Prophets*, p. 36), an indication of their oneness and equality.

Presuming God the Father to possess the fullness of the Godhead, Paul declares that in Christ dwells "the fulness of the Godhead bodily" (Col. 2:9) and that Christ is the express image of the Father's person (Heb. 1:3). In other words, there is perfect equality between the Father and the Son.

In harmony with Scripture, Ellen White's statement in *Early Writings* describes the Father and Son as distinct divine individuals, a truth she would emphasize many times. Here are a few examples: "From eternity there was a complete unity between the Father and the Son. They were two, yet little short of being identical; two in individuality, yet one in spirit, and heart, and character" (*Youth's Instructor*, Dec. 16, 1897). "There is a personal God, the Father; there is a personal Christ, the Son" (*Review and Herald*, Nov. 8, 1898). "The seventeenth chapter of John speaks plainly regarding the personality of God and of Christ, and of their relation to each other. 'Father, the hour is come,' Christ said: 'glorify thy Son, that thy Son also may glorify thee.' [John 17:23, 3, 5–11 quoted.] Here is personality, and individuality" (Ms. 124, 1903, in *Seventh-day Adventist Bible Commentary*, vol. 5, p. 1145). "The Scriptures clearly indicate the relation between God and Christ, and they bring to view as clearly the personality and individuality of each.... [Hebrews 1:1–5 quoted.] God is the Father of Christ; Christ is the Son of God. To Christ has been given

Was Ellen White Really a Semi-Arian? 17

an exalted position. He has been made equal with the Father" (*Testimonies for the Church*, vol. 8, p. 268, written in 1904). "The Lord Jesus Christ, the only begotten Son of the Father, is truly God in infinity, but not in personality" (Ms. 116, 1905, in *Upward Look*, p. 367). "While they are one in purpose, and one in mind, yet in personality they are two" (*Review and Herald*, Aug. 15, 1907). It should be noted that Ellen White used the term "personality" as we would now use "personhood."

Both Father and Son possess the fullness of the Godhead bodily. That the Son is the express image of the Father's person (Heb. 1:3) signifies clear equality and unity between the two. How else could He truly be the express image of the Father if He were of a different nature and substance?

Other translations describe the Son's image this way:

- "the very image of his substance"
  (*American Standard Version*)
- "an exact representation of his very being"
  (*Rotherham*)
- "flawless expression of the nature of God"
  (*Phillips*)

Quotation Number 2

The Father's Form

Following is the next statement presented as evidence that Ellen White held semi-Arian views:

> I saw a throne, and on it sat the Father and the Son. I gazed on Jesus' countenance and admired His lovely person. The Father's person I could not behold, for a cloud of glorious light covered Him. I asked Jesus if His Father had a form like Himself. He said He had, but I could not behold it, for said He, "If you should once behold the glory of His person you would cease to exist." (*Early Writings*, p. 54)

Was Ellen White Really a Semi-Arian?

Based on this quotation, some have asserted that Ellen White presented Christ and the Father as distinct individuals and not as one. They have also asserted that Mrs. White would not have written the statement this way if she saw the Father and Son as existing in a single substance. Thus, they conclude that Ellen White was a semi-Arian in her early ministry, some distance in belief from her later Trinitarianism.[4]

In the vision, Ellen White could only see and admire Jesus and not the Father. This was because a cloud of glorious light covered the Father. Had she been able to see the Father, she would have ceased to exist. Does this mean that there is a substantive difference in nature between Christ and the Father? Should we interpret this vision as being semi-Arian and classify Ellen White's position as such?

To properly interpret this statement, we need to consider the context. Without it, we are prone to unfair and mistaken conclusions.

---

4. No other of Mrs. White's statement epitomizes her Trinitarian views better than her statement in *The Desire of Ages*, "*In* Christ is *life, original, unborrowed, underived*" (p. 530). This statement was adapted from *Signs of the Times*, April 8, 1897. Ellen White, in her presentation of truth, was guided by God. When she noted befitting and apt words, descriptions or expressions used by other well-known authors, she did not see it a problem to adapt these for her own writing. Her use of this phrasing is a double blessing. Besides helping her describe her understanding of the subject, it demonstrates that, Seventh-day Adventists are in harmony with other Christians on these fundamental points of faith, avoiding unnecessary prejudice. We should not be surprised to find the italicized words in this quotation having originated with John Cumming, *Sabbath Evening Readings. St. John*, page 6.

Before the throne were two companies of people, one was interested and the other was careless. Ellen White wrote:

> Those who were bowed before the throne would offer up their prayers and look to Jesus; then He would look to His Father, and appear pleading with Him.... I saw the Father rise from His throne, and in a flaming chariot go into the holy of holies within the veil, and sit down. (*Early Writings*, pp. 54, 55)

The question arises: Is this a vision depicting a scene before the foundations of the earth were laid? No, definitely not! Christ is not pictured here in His eternal glory, equal with the Father. In this vision, Christ and His Father are presented as sitting on the throne *in the heavenly sanctuary.* Before the creation of the earth and before sin, there was no sanctuary in heaven in which Christ mediated on humanity's behalf, for there was no need. Only after the fall of man was such a sanctuary instituted. The vision in *Early Writings* depicts human beings praying and looking up to Jesus, who is pleading with the Father on their behalf. The vision provides a clear picture of the plan of salvation, with Christ acting as Mediator between fallen humanity and the Father.[5]

It goes without saying that, as long as Christ is ministering in the heavenly sanctuary, the plan of salvation is still in force. The Bible teaches us that Christ humbled Himself to save humankind. In this vision, Christ is still functioning as humanity's Mediator. He has not yet laid down His intercessory role or clothed Himself with glory, which He will only do when He leaves the sanctuary and returns to Earth to bring His faithful followers back to the heavenly Jerusalem.

Was Ellen White Really a Semi-Arian? 21

In representing the heavenly aspect of the plan of salvation, Christ is always presented in His humbled state. The depiction in this vision offers no real problem. Of course the Father is greater in the plan of salvation than the Son (John 14:28). The Father did not take upon Him the role of Mediator. There is only one name by which we must be saved (Acts 4:12) and only one mediator between God and men" (1 Tim. 2:5)—Jesus.

Let us reiterate what Ellen White related in this second statement: it was the question she asked and the answer she received in the vision. She does not explain here what she believed about the Trinity or the Godhead. It is not right to attribute her description to a supposed semi-Arian understanding.

---

5. In fact, we should note that Ellen White's vision depicts events that occurred at the time of the Great Disappointment, when Christ did not come to this earth but to his Father, "the Ancient of Days," as shown in Daniel 7:13. In chapter 28 of *The Great Controversy*, Ellen White identified "the Ancient of Days" as "the source of all being, and the fountain of all law" (*The Great Controversy*, p. 479). In the New Testament, Paul described this scene in 1 Corinthians 15:24–28. God the Father puts all things under the authority (or "feet") of His Son until the end comes, and "then shall the Son also himself be subject" to His Father. All three accounts portray God the Father and Christ as two distinct entities. Because Christ is the Son of God, He inherits all things from his Father—including His name. "Jehovah is the name given to Christ" (*Signs of the Times*, May 3, 1899). Paul referred to this in Philippians 2:9: "Wherefore God also hath highly exalted him, and given him a name which is above every name." In Ellen White's vision in *Early Writings*, pages 54, 55, God the Father moves from the holy place to the most holy place on the antitypical day of atonement of 1844; Jesus the Son goes to Him to receive His kingdom and dominion. These same two persons are also spoken of in Revelation, when "the kingdoms of this world ... "become the kingdoms of our Lord and of his Christ" (Rev. 11:15) at the end of all things, there will only be "the throne of God and the Lamb" (Rev. 22:1, 3; cf. Rev. 4:9; 5:6).

QUOTATION NUMBER 3

Breathing Upon People the Holy Ghost

In the opinion of some, the following statement should also be regarded as evidence of Ellen White's supposed semi-Arian views:

> Those who rose up with Jesus would send up their faith to Him in the holiest, and pray, "My Father, give us Thy Spirit." Then Jesus would breathe upon them the Holy Ghost. In that breath was light, power, and much love, joy, and peace. (*Early Writings*, p. 55)

Was Ellen White Really a Semi-Arian?

In this statement, Ellen White describes Jesus' conveyance of the Holy Spirit to human beings by His breathing on them. Assuming this representation to be semi-Arian, some use it to say that Ellen White espoused anti-Trinitarian views in her early Adventist experience.

Yet, let us not forget who chose to give this representation to Ellen White in vision. It was God—not Mrs. White. Neither should we forget that there is a similar representation in Scripture, when Jesus "breathed on" the disciples and said to them, "Receive ye the Holy Ghost" (John 20:22). Thus, if Ellen White's depiction of Jesus breathing the Holy Spirit on people gives reason to accuse Ellen White of semi-Arianism, it also gives reason to accuse the writers of the Scriptures of teaching the same. Yet, that does not make sense.

Should we not take the breathing of Christ as symbolic, in light of the story of the Creation, in which God *breathed* into man's nostrils the breath of life and man became a living soul (Gen. 2:7)? Is it not in this way that Jesus breathed the Holy Spirit upon the disciples—as a re-creating source of life and divine power and authority? We conclude: this vision has nothing to do with semi-Arianism.[6]

---

6. Note also that there is an additional detail in this vision. Ellen White wrote: "A light would come from the Father to the Son and from the Son to the praying company" (*Early Writings*, p. 55). This is the sequence described in Scripture as well: "The Spirit of truth, which proceedeth from the Father" "whom I will send unto you from the Father" (John 15:26) for "God hath sent forth the Spirit of his Son into your hearts" (Gal. 4:6).

QUOTATION NUMBER 4

The Council Between Father and Son

Another statement that is used to support the view that Ellen White was semi-Arian in belief is the following:

> I saw the lovely Jesus, and beheld an expression of sympathy and sorrow upon his countenance. Soon I saw him approach the exceeding bright light which enshrouded the Father. Said my accompanying angel, "He is in close converse with his Father." The anxiety of the angels seemed to be intense while Jesus was communing with his Father. Three times he was shut in by the glorious light about the Father, and the third time he came from the Father we could see his person; and his countenance was calm, free from all perplexity and trouble, and shone with loveliness, such as words cannot express. He then made known to the angelic choir that a way of escape had been made for lost man; that he had been pleading with his Father, and had obtained his consent to give his life a ransom, to bear their sins, and take the sentence of death upon himself ... (*Supplement to the Christian Experience and Views of Ellen G. White*, p. 47)

Was Ellen White Really a Semi-Arian?

Some allege this statement to teach that Christ is very different from the Father and completely separate from Him. They allege, from His being the only One shrouded in glory, that all power and authority is in the Father's hands while Jesus is only of lesser importance. Here again, we need to remember that this is not a confession of Ellen White's personal belief or understanding of the Trinity. It is unfair to force this upon the depiction. Ellen White has only stated faithfully what she saw and heard, without any word of her own opinion or interpretation. If this vision is to be branded as semi-Arian, then Ellen White is not responsible for it, for she was not the source and originator of the vision. It was God who gave it; it is He who is responsible for its content.

Why does this vision depict such difference between Christ and the Father? Is it because of semi-Arianism?

Once humankind succumbed to sin, the plan of redemption required Christ's condescension. Christ could only plead for fallen humankind as Mediator after becoming a human and shedding His blood. Could Christ have successfully pled with His Father on fallen humanity's behalf from His eternal glory? No—the context of the vision portrays humanity as having already fallen into sin. Only with humanity and divinity combined could Christ rescue fallen man. Only as He had taken our place could Christ successfully plead for sinful humankind and the Father view sinful humans with favor. Only through Christ's humiliation, death, and righteousness could God carry out His plan to save fallen humanity.

Consequently, as soon as humans sinned, there was a Saviour and the plan of salvation was put into operation.

As humanity's slain Lamb and Mediator, Jesus stepped in between God and sinners, taking the position of fallen humanity and becoming fallen humanity's sin bearer. He did so, as it were, in advance of His death on Calvary's cross but by virtue of the same. In anticipation of His incarnation, He appeared in Old Testament times in human form (Gen. 18; 32:24–30). It is no wonder that Ellen White saw Christ in this vision with a visible form, pleading with the Father. Since Christ was the Lamb "slain from the foundation of this world" (Rev. 13:8), He officiated, before the Incarnation, as a true and faithful Mediator.

The decision that Jesus would die in our place was already agreed upon in eternity—before the foundation of the earth (Heb. 10:5, 7).[7] According to the vision, before God implemented the plan of salvation, the angels saw Christ in close communion with His Father, approaching the Father three times. Christ afterward told them that a way of escape had been made and that He had obtained the Father's consent to give His life. Some people argue that this cannot be a representation of what actually happened because the heavenly agreement was already made before the creation of the world. Of course, the angels had

---

7. In *The Desire of Ages*, page 23, Ellen White again emphasized the Son's choice in becoming man's substitute: "*Nearly two thousand years ago, a voice of mysterious import was heard* in heaven, *from the throne* of God, 'Lo, I come.' 'Sacrifice and offering Thou wouldest not, but a body hast Thou prepared Me.... Lo, I come (in the volume of the Book it is written of Me,) to do Thy will, O God.*' [Heb. 10:5, 7]." We find the italicized words also in Heman Humphrey's introduction to John Harris's book, *The Great Teacher*, page xiii. See also *Review and Herald*, November 11, 1890, and *The Youth's Instructor*, November 21, 1895.

Was Ellen White Really a Semi-Arian?

not been present in the heavenly council when the plan of salvation was originally agreed upon. They did not know all that God had planned (Matt. 24:36). Perhaps this meeting could possibly be best described as a dramatic "re-enactment" of the original "counsel of peace" (Zech. 6:13) for the benefit of the on-looking angels as the plan of redemption now required that Christ take on a new role. The drama of Christ's approaching the Father three times and of the Father's consent to Christ's condescension was for their benefit.[8]

The anxiety of the angels at man's fall seemed intense. They were deeply moved, and, no wonder, for they were now witnesses of the initialization of the plan of salvation. Saddened that their beloved Leader would have to suffer, the angels offered their lives as a sacrifice for humankind. Christ told them that would not work. A created being could never pay the price to save fallen humanity (*Spirit of Prophecy*, vol. 1, p. 50). As the Father and Son retired from their council, the plan of salvation was formally in place.

What the angelic hosts took in with great interest signified the value that God placed on man's redemption.

---

8. It is also for the benefit of the readers of her account of the vision, to show the love of the Father and the Son. The Father demonstrated that He "*so* loved" the fallen race by giving His Son (John 3:16). Ellen White emphasized how much God gave in reporting what she heard in vision: "Said the angel, 'Think ye that the Father yielded up his dearly beloved Son without a struggle? No, no.' It was even a struggle with the God of heaven, whether to let guilty man perish, or to give His darling Son to die for them" (*Supplement to the Christian Experience and Views of Ellen G. White*, p. 48). Christ's love is seen in His willingly giving Himself as the sacrifice for the redemption of humanity (Gal. 2:20; 1:4; Eph. 5:25; 1 Tim. 2:6; Titus 2:14; Heb. 9:14).

Christ pleaded with the Father for His consent. This reveals the unity and full co-operation between Father and Son and left no room for the angels to doubt that the plan of salvation was being executed without Heaven's full agreement. They were witnesses that the Father had endorsed the condescension of their beloved Leader and were convinced that there was perfect agreement between the two that this was the only way to save fallen humanity.

In the context of God's plan of salvation, Christ indeed is, because of His condescension, lesser than the Father, though not in His divine nature (John 14:28). There is no difference between the divine nature of the Father and of the Son. The self-existent, immortal, quickening life that is in the Father is also in the Son because, as Jesus has said, the Father gave it to Him (John 5:26) and made His Son a quickening Spirit like Himself (1 Cor. 15:45).

As a golden chain, God's plan of salvation runs throughout the entire Bible, and we find several passages, such as John 14:28, in which Christ is presented as lesser than the Father. In God's plan of salvation, Father and Son have different roles. We could say, perhaps, that the Father took the leading role of director, while Christ took the role of executor, and the Holy Spirit of fulfilling Christ's accomplished work. Ellen White wrote: "The Godhead was stirred with pity for the race, and the Father, the Son, and the Holy Spirit gave Themselves to the working out of the plan of redemption" (*Counsels on Health*, p. 222).

This brief statement, written in 1899, implies that the Godhead is composed of the Father, Son, and Holy Spirit, and that these three were stirred with pity for the human race. In the sentence just before this one, Ellen White quoted John 3:16, identifying the Father as the One who was stirred by pity and love for the world to give His only begotten Son. Thus, the plan was devised and agreed upon through the close communion of the Father and the Son. Yet, now, after the fall of man, the Father formally committed Himself, His Son, and His Spirit to the fulfillment of a plan that He had already made with His Son.

That Christ is seen in the vision, unequal in position and glory with the Father, is not owing to any difference between them explained by Semi-Arianism. No, in God's plan of redemption, we behold the humbling of Christ, not the humbling of the Father. It was Christ who "emptied himself" (Phil. 4:7, *Revised Standard Version*). No wonder Ellen White saw Christ's form and not that of the Father. The Father was gloriously enshrouded, while He emanated all power and authority.

The cross of Christ is the center of man's salvation and the focus of and Christ's great condescension and submission to the Father. When the plan of salvation ends at the *final coronation*, all men will behold Christ *fully glorified*. At that time, the Father will exalt His Son, and every knee will bow and every tongue will "confess that Jesus Christ is Lord, to the glory of God the Father" (Phil. 2:11).

Salvation, which came through Christ's condescension, was to rescue humankind, not the angels. Thus, at His ascension, while the plan was still in play, Christ was glorified amidst angels. "When the great sacrifice had been consummated, Christ ascended on high, refusing the adoration of angels until He had presented the request, 'I will that they also, whom Thou hast given Me, be with Me where I am.' John 17:24. Then with inexpressible love and power came forth the answer from the Father's throne: 'Let all the angels of God worship Him.' Hebrews 1:6. Not a stain rested upon Jesus. His humiliation ended, His sacrifice completed, there was given unto Him a name that is above every name" (*The Great Controversy*, pp. 501, 502). But His role in behalf of humanity did not end there. At the end of the thousand years, however, when the plan of salvation comes to its end, then the whole of humanity will be involved in Christ's exaltation and glorification.

Christ ascended to heaven, "enthroned amidst the adoration of the angels" and glorified "with the glory which He had with the Father from all eternity" (*Acts of the Apostles*, pp. 38, 39). The price for humankind's rescue was paid, Satan was defeated, and death was conquered. Nonetheless, the plan of salvation did not then end, for we still live in a sinful world. The great controversy between good and evil rages on, and those who died in faith are still dead. The saints are not yet gathered into God's kingdom, and Christ still ministers in the heavenly sanctuary on behalf of humanity. As long as He is carrying out His mediatorial role, He is depicted in Scripture in His humbled state. Says Hebrews 2:17: "Wherefore in all things it behoved him to be made like unto his brethren, that he might be a merciful and faithful high priest in things pertaining to God, to make reconciliation for the sins of the people." Thus, the humbled state of Christ, like unto His brethren, makes Him a merciful and faithful high priest, and that is how we see Him as He pleads with the Father (Rev. 1:12, 13).

At the end of the plan of salvation, however, as the thousand years come to a close and the wicked are about to be judged and destroyed, then will Christ be *fully glorified* and invested with *supreme majesty and power*, occupying His *rightful position*. Ellen White describes the scene: "In the presence of the assembled inhabitants of earth and heaven the final coronation of the Son of God takes place. And now, invested with supreme majesty and power, the King of kings pronounces sentence upon the rebels against His government and executes justice upon those who have transgressed His law and oppressed His people" (*The Great Controversy*, p. 666). Then can it be said, "The hour has come when Christ occupies His rightful position and is glorified above principalities and powers and every name that is named" (*The Great Controversy*, p. 671). Thus, Christ's humiliation in the scope of God's plan of redemption will be ended and it will be as it was before sin entered this world.

The preceding sentence of the quoted one on page 671 in *The Great Controversy* reads: "Before the universe has been clearly presented the great sacrifice made by *the Father and the Son*." As it was before sin, so it will be after sin. The Father and Son entered into the "counsel of peace" that was "between them both" (Zech. 6:13). In the end, the Father and Son reign supreme. Jesus promised that those who overcome will sit with Him in His throne as He overcame and is set down with His Father on His throne (Rev. 3:21). Ellen White completes the description of the scene by saying, "The glory of God and the Lamb floods the Holy City with unfading light. The redeemed walk in the sunless glory of perpetual day" and with the words of Revelation 21:22: "I saw no temple therein: for the Lord God Almighty and the Lamb are the temple of it" (*The Great Controversy*, p. 676). Two pages later she says: "And the years of eternity, as they roll, will bring richer and still more glorious revelations of *God* and of *Christ....* 'And every creature which is in heaven, and on the earth, and under the earth, and such as are in the sea, and all that are in them, heard I saying, Blessing, and honor, and glory, and power, be unto *Him that sitteth upon the throne*, and *unto the Lamb* for ever and ever.' Revelation 5:13" (*The Great Controversy*, p. 678, emphasis supplied).

Thus, as the plan of salvation draws to a close, Christ is restored to full equality and complete oneness with the Father, and all things revert to what they had been before sin entered the world. What a wonderful and blessed finale for God's plan of redemption!

The limited condescension of Christ, we conclude, which lasts as long as the plan of salvation is in effect, was necessary for the redemption of fallen humanity. We miss the point of the description in Ellen White's vision if we interpret as semi-Arianism Christ's being temporarily less than the Father.

Ellen White's early visions are neither contradictory nor unbiblical. Understood within their rightful context, they contribute valuable insights about God's plan of salvation.

QUOTATION NUMBER 5

The Shared Throne of Father and Son

Assuming that Ellen White's early visions were semi-Arian, some argue that Mrs. White portrayed Jesus without glory because, in her naïve view of the Godhead, she could not imagine Jesus sharing the Father's glory. Building on this argument, they assert that Ellen White began moving away from semi-Arianism toward Trinitarianism some time around 1890, as evidenced by statements she then made. Her turning point in belief is supposedly illustrated in the following statement, published in 1890:

> The Son of God shared the Father's throne, and the glory of the eternal, self-existent One encircled both. (*Patriarchs and Prophets*, p. 36)

Does this statement really illustrate Ellen White's renunciation of semi-Arian views and her embracing of Trinitarianism around 1890? If we look at the context of this sentence, we see perfect harmony and a clear confirmation of how correct Ellen White always was in her concept of the Father and the Son. The sentence about the sharing of the Father's throne occurs in "Why Was Sin Permitted?" a chapter that describes Satan's rebellion in heaven *before* the creation of humankind.

This indicates that there was no plan of salvation in operation at that time, and Christ's actual condescension was yet to take place. It is no wonder that Christ is pictured as sharing the Father's throne, glory, and authority. The context, which begins on page 34, says:

> The Sovereign of the universe was not alone in His work of beneficence. He had an associate—a co-worker who could appreciate His purposes, and could share His joy in giving happiness to created beings. (*Patriarchs and Prophets*)

Yes, God did indeed have an associate who could appreciate His purposes, but they were still the purposes of "the Sovereign of the universe." In the sentence that follows, Ellen White quotes John 1:1, which identifies the Sovereign of the universe as God the Father and His associate as the Word who "was with God" (John 1:1). Mrs. White then declares: "Christ, the Word, the only begotten of God, was one with the eternal Father" (*Patriarchs and Prophets*, p. 34). How was Christ one with the eternal Father? She answers: He was "one in nature, in character, in purpose—the only being that could enter into all the counsels and purposes of God." Mrs. White then quotes Isaiah and Micah for the names given to the incarnate Son of God that depict His eternal divinity: "'His name shall be called Wonderful, Counselor, The mighty God, The everlasting Father, The Prince of Peace.' Isaiah 9:6. His 'goings forth have been from of old, from everlasting.' Micah 5:2." Christ is indeed the eternal Son from everlasting. There is no indication of inequality.

Nevertheless, in the context of the founding of the earth and the activation of the plan of redemption, Ellen White says: "And the Son of God declares concerning Himself: 'The Lord possessed Me in the beginning of His way, before his works of old. I was set up from everlasting.... When He appointed the foundations of the earth: then I was by Him.' Proverbs 8:22–30."[9]

Ellen White then identifies "the Son" as "the anointed of God," an allusion to Psalm 2:2; 45:7; and Hebrews 1:9. This identification harmonizes with the description she had given of that which Lucifer coveted—"the glory with which the infinite Father had invested His Son" (*Patriarchs and Prophets*, p. 35).

Once again we can say that Ellen White is in full agreement with the Scriptures, which say that the Father loves the Son and has given all things into his hand

---

9. The Son states that "the Lord" (which, in this context, means the Sovereign of the universe—God, the eternal Father) "possessed" Him (Hebrew *qanah*, which in Qal means "to get, acquire, or obtain"). The first usage of the verb, in Genesis 4:1, 2, is translated "gotten," which is the root of the name *Qayin*, or "Cain."

(John 3:35; 13:3; Matt. 11:27; Heb. 1:2). Ellen White's 1890 statement affirms the perfect equality of Christ and the Father before the creation of this world, as they shared the same throne and glory. It has nothing to do with any supposed abandonment of semi-Arianism. Rather, it delivers the sound biblical teaching that Christ humbled Himself in order to secure the salvation of humankind (Phil. 2:5–8).

The plan of redemption was not initialized at Christ's incarnation. Christ had already humbled Himself when our first parents fell into sin. Before the creation, the Father and Son were in agreement that Christ would assume a mediatorial role in a humbled state to save humankind. He was "the lamb slain *from the foundation of the world*" (Rev. 13:8, emphasis supplied).

Quotation Number 6

The Father's Ordaining of Christ's Equality

That the Father is the sole Supreme God and that Jesus is far lower in status is also supposedly reflected in the following statement, a supposed indication of Ellen White's semi-Arianism:

> The great Creator assembled the heavenly host, that he might in the presence of all the angels confer special honor upon his Son.... The Father then made known that it was ordained by himself that Christ, his Son, should be equal with himself; so that wherever was the presence of his Son, it was as his own presence.... His Son would carry out His will and His purposes, but would do nothing of himself alone. The Father's will would be fulfilled in him. (*Spirit of Prophecy,* vol. 1, pp. 17, 18)

Should we indeed read this passage in terms of semi-Arianism, or is it making another point?

The statement is part of a vision, which, taken in context, explains why the heavenly host were assembled—it was to confer special honor upon the Son. Does the context portray the Father as the Supreme God and the Son as far less and not one with the Father, as some assert? Ellen White wrote on the same page: "Jesus, God's dear Son, had the pre-eminence over all the angelic host. He was one with the Father before the angels were created" (*Spirit of Prophecy*, vol. 1, p. 17). Mrs. White confirms that, before this assembly of the heavenly hosts, Christ held pre-eminence over the angels and had already been one with the Father from times eternal. Thus, equality and oneness with the Father and the Son did not start at this ceremony, but were merely *confirmed* then by the Father.

Ellen White wrote: "Satan was envious of Christ, and gradually assumed command which devolved on Christ alone" (*Spirit of Prophecy*, vol. 1, p. 17). The situation was certainly confusing to the angels. Christ was known to them as "their exalted and loving Commander" (*Spiritual Gifts*, vol. 3, p. 37), yet Lucifer disputed Christ's position and influenced the angels to make a choice. So who was their true commander? Was it Christ, or was it Lucifer? To settle this question, the Father assembled the heavenly host to make the matter clear by conferring special honor upon His Son and confirming Christ to be the rightful commander.[10]

On the following page, Ellen White says: "But Christ was acknowledged sovereign of Heaven, his power and authority to be the same as that of God himself" (*Spirit of Prophecy*, vol. 1, p. 18). If Christ is one with the Father and if He shares equal power and authority with Him, there is no reason to infer semi-Arianism in this passage.

Note Ellen White's description of the same event, made two decades later:

> There had been no change in the position or authority of Christ. Lucifer's envy and misrepresentation and his claims to equality with Christ had made necessary a statement of the true position of the Son of God; but this had been the same from the beginning. Many of the angels were, however, blinded by Lucifer's deceptions. (*Patriarchs and Prophets*, p. 38)

This later statement is in harmony with Ellen White's earlier statement, "He was one with the Father before the angels were created." Neither statement indicates a change in Christ's position or authority, for those have been the same from the beginning. Semi-Arianism is not reflected in this passage.

---

10. A few short quotations make clear that Christ is next to God and that Lucifer was next to Christ. Michael the archangel, who is Christ (*Spirit of Prophecy*, vol. 1, p. 342; *Spiritual Gifts*, vol. 4a, p. 57), stood at the right hand of God: "He was next to God in the heavenly courts" (Letter 48, 1902, in *Notebook Leaflets from the Elmshaven Library*, vol. 1, p. 114). Though Christ had created all the heavenly host, He shared honor with Lucifer, "who, next to Christ, had been most honored of God" (*The Great Controversy*, p. 493). Gabriel is now "the angel who stands next in honor to the Son of God." He said to Daniel: " 'There is none that holdeth with me in these things, but Michael [Christ] your Prince.' Daniel 10:21" (*The Desire of Ages*, p. 99).

Some may conclude from Ellen White's description that the angels did not know that Christ was equal with the Father and needed God to call a special assembly to inform them of this truth. Such a conclusion is unwarranted. It was not because of the angels' ignorance of Christ's equality with the Father, but because, in his envy and jealousy of Christ, Satan had sowed uncertainty and doubt among the angels concerning Christ's position and authority. Many angels were blinded by Lucifer's deceptions. That is the reason the Father needed to confer honor upon the Son at the assembly. It was to clarify the true position of the Son of God and remove any excuse for following the deceptive misrepresentations of Satan. The Father made plain that it was Christ and not Lucifer who was equal with Him.

Others take Ellen White's 1870 statement as evidence that Ellen White believed early on that Christ is not equal with the Father by nature but only by the Father's ordaining. Can that idea be substantiated by more than vague inferences? There is no need to wonder if this is true. As was mentioned before, on the same page Ellen White says that Christ "was one with the Father before the angels were created" (*Spirit of Prophecy*, vol. 1, p. 17). How can Christ truly be one with the Father without sharing the Father's nature? How could He become our Redeemer if He were not fully divine? Declaring that He was already one with the Father, how could Mrs. White have believed that Christ was equal with the Father by commission only? The semi-Arian view just does not make sense.

If we assert such things without clear and sound evidence sustained by the context and entrench ourselves behind disconnected utterances construed to suit our own imperfect suppositions, do we not line up with the enemy of truth? Wanting to be equal with God, Lucifer disputed Christ's equality with the Father and foisted upon the angels a false view of Christ. This was why the Father decreed that not Lucifer but Christ is equal with Himself. Lucifer, who became known as the Devil and Satan, was cast from heaven to earth along with his deluded angels. Because he still hates the Son of God, he continues to try to implant a distorted view of Christ in human minds.

The perverted view that Satan particularly wishes to implant is that Christ is not truly the only begotten Son of God, equal with the Father: "This fact the [fallen] angels would obscure, that Christ was the only begotten Son of God" (Letter 42, 1910, in *This Day With God*, p. 128). Yet, Ellen White wrote: "His Son would carry out His will and His purposes, but would do nothing of himself alone" (*Spirit of Prophecy*, vol. 1, p. 17). Thus, Scripture stresses the unity and complete harmony between Christ and the Father. There was no need for the angels to have any doubt about the falsity of Lucifer's allegations, as he sought to usurp Christ's position. Lucifer's covert takeover of God's government was the Father's motivation for affirming Christ as being one with Himself. The context answers an emphatic "No!" to the question, "Is Christ's equality with the Father only by decree and not by nature?"

Only the reality of Christ's being the Son of God, begotten from the Father from eternity guarantees the divinity of Christ by nature—an absolutely independent self-existent yet co-eternal second person in perfect union with the Godhead.

Regarding the Father's ordaining of Christ's equality, it should be stressed again that Ellen White did not present her own views. Nor did she invent or devise the things that she described. She was shown these things by God and guided by the Holy Spirit. If we, nevertheless, persist in holding onto our own peculiar views and impose semi-Arianism on her statements, we misuse her writings and impugn God, the source of what she described.

Chapter 2

ELLEN WHITE AND THE HOLY SPIRIT

Some claim that Ellen White did not recognize the Holy Spirit as a Person until later in her prophetic career. They do this in part based on a statement she made in 1873.

QUOTATION NUMBER 1

Christ's Baptism and the "Beams of Glory"

The heavens were opened, and beams of glory rested upon the Son of God and assumed the form of a dove, in appearance like burnished gold. The dove-like form was emblematical of the meekness and gentleness of Christ. (*Review and Herald*, Jan. 1, 1873)

In this statement, Ellen White does not expressly mention the Holy Spirit.[11] Rather than connecting the dove-like form with the Holy Spirit, she connected it with "beams of glory" and the meekness and gentleness of Christ. Because this seems to be a deliberate avoidance of the Holy Spirit, some have concluded that Ellen White still did not believe in the personhood of the Spirit. It is amazing how differently people can sometimes read a passage!

Some of these same people consider Ellen White's connecting of these symbols to be a strange commentary. Yet, is it so strange? It would be if Ellen White were declaring that the heavenly dove was not the Holy Spirit, for that would contradict Scripture. Yet, Ellen White does not say anything like that. She explains that the heavens were opened and beams of glory rested upon the Son, assumed the form of a dove, which appeared like burnished gold. The Bible tells us that God is light, and

---

11. In an earlier statement, Mrs. White outlined the role of all three members of the Godhead in this scene: "Angels of God hovered over the scene of his baptism, and the Holy Spirit descended in the shape of a dove, and lighted upon him, and as the people stood greatly amazed, with their eyes fastened upon him, the FATHER's voice was heard from heaven, saying, Thou art my beloved SON, in thee I am well pleased" (*Spiritual Gifts*, vol. 1, pp. 28, 29). The Spirit's agency is depicted in a scene immediately following: "After the baptism of JESUS in Jordan, he was led by the Spirit into the wilderness, to be tempted of the Devil. The Holy Spirit had fitted him for that special scene of fierce temptations. Forty days he was tempted of the Devil, and in those days he ate nothing. Everything around JESUS was unpleasant, from which human nature would be led to shrink. He was with the wild beasts, and the Devil, in a desolate, lonely place. I saw that the SON of GOD was pale and emaciated through fasting and suffering. But his course was marked out, and he must fulfill the work he came to do" (*Spiritual Gifts*, vol. 1, p. 31).

so is the Holy Spirit. There is no darkness in Him at all, and Christ's baptism was certainly not a manifestation of darkness. Rather, it was as Ellen White said, an occasion during which "beams of glory rested upon the Son of God."

It is true that Ellen White did not mention the dove-like form as being the Holy Spirit in this particular statement, yet is that an indication that she did not believe that the dove-like form was the Holy Spirit or that she was deliberately avoiding mentioning the Holy Spirit?

Again, the context provides the answer. Farther on in the article Ellen White quotes John 1:32, 33:

> "And John bare record, saying, I saw the Spirit descending from heaven like a dove, and it abode upon him. And I knew him not: but he that sent me to baptize with water, the same said unto me, Upon whom thou shalt see the Spirit descending, and remaining on him, the same is he which baptizeth with the Holy Ghost."

Would Ellen White have quoted this unambiguous passage if she were deliberately avoiding the Holy Spirit or if she did not support what the text says about the Holy Spirit? How odd that would be—particularly in light of what she said in the article farther down: "Christ virtually says, On the bank of Jordan the heavens were opened before me, and the Spirit descended like a dove upon me." Without a doubt, Ellen White acknowledged the dove-like form as the Holy Spirit. Otherwise, she would not have made this statement.

Was the dove-like form not a symbol of the meekness and gentleness of Christ? Several sources support this symbolic or emblematic meaning of the dove. The Bible speaks of being "harmless as doves" (Matt. 10:16). Other versions translate the word for "harmless" as "innocent," "blameless," or "guileless." When the Holy Spirit descended upon Christ like a dove, as the symbol of meekness and gentleness, it pointed to the meekness and gentleness of Christ. One with the Holy Spirit, Christ's life was led by the Spirit (see Luke 4:1).

Reflecting upon Christ's baptism, we note that the Father was present at this important event and declared from the open heavens, "This is My beloved Son, in whom I am well pleased" (Matt. 3:17). Twenty-five years later, Ellen White enlarged upon this event, maintaining consistency with the disputed description. She wrote: "And John, yielding, led the Saviour down into the Jordan, and buried Him beneath the water. 'And straightway coming up out of the water,' Jesus 'saw the heavens opened, and the Spirit like a dove descending upon Him.' " Two paragraphs later, she writes:

> Upon coming up out of the water, Jesus bowed in prayer on the river bank.... The Saviour's glance seems to penetrate heaven as He pours out His soul in prayer.... Never before have the angels listened to such a prayer. They are eager to bear to their loved Commander a message of assurance and comfort. But no; *the Father Himself will answer* the petition of His Son. *Direct from the throne issue the beams of His glory.* The heavens are opened, and upon the Saviour's head descends a dovelike form of purest light,—fit emblem of Him, the meek and lowly One. (*The Desire of Ages*, pp. 111, 112)

Presenting greater detail here, Ellen White, explains that it is not just light that shines upon Jesus, but the Father's glory, shining directly from His throne. The Father declares, "This is My beloved Son," and the audible manifestation of His presence is heard. The Father's glory descends upon His Son's head, and the visible manifestation of His presence is seen. Note how all three members of the Godhead in unity were present at this wonderful event. Christ, as the world's Redeemer, was baptized, and the Father's glory encircled Him, while the Holy Spirit rested upon Him.

Ellen White wrote on the same page: "As the glory of God encircled Him, and the voice from heaven was heard, John recognized the token which God had promised. He knew that it was the world's Redeemer whom he had baptized. The Holy Spirit rested upon him …" Thus we see complete unity between the Father, the Son, and the Holy Spirit. Jesus spoke of the Spirit of His Father and assured His disciples that it is "the Spirit of your Father which speaketh in you" (Matt. 10:20).

QUOTATION NUMBER 2

The Spirit's Personhood

Some people are of the opinion that it was not until the year 1897 that Ellen White recognized the Holy Spirit as the third person of the Godhead. This recognition, they claim, came to her like a bolt out of the blue. The following statement, published in 1897, is supposed to mark this turning point in Mrs. White's understanding.

> The prince of the power of evil can only be held in check by the power of God in the third person of the Godhead, the Holy Spirit. (*Special Testimonies*, Series A, No. 10, p. 37)

Ellen White and the Holy Spirit

At long last, they say, she recognized that the Holy Spirit is a person and is, in fact, a member of the Godhead. They surmise from this that Ellen White did not give the Holy Spirit His rightful place during her supposed semi-Arian period and that she only came to terms with His personhood and deity in 1897.[12] Thus, they assume that it took Ellen White nearly fifty years to accept what the Bible always taught about the Holy Spirit.

It is clear that these are, once again, unproved assertions. If the Spirit of Prophecy is a gift from God, which we believe it is, then we should value this gift and not neglect or underestimate it or misrepresent it through unsound suggestions, assertions, or accusations. Doing so exhibits a disloyal lack of trust in God, who, in His wisdom chose to bless the church during this unparalleled time of the end with this valuable gift.

Typifying Ellen White's insight about the Holy Spirit in the way it is done here is unwarranted. The fact that Ellen White did not present, in her early ministry, a detailed statement about the personhood of the Holy Spirit does not mean that she did not believe in His personhood or that she cherished a mistaken view of the Holy Spirit. That would only be an unsubstantiated supposition, because none of her early statements are out of harmony with the teaching of the Bible. Of course, in her early writing there

---

12. A slightly earlier use of the phrase "the third person of the Godhead" is found in Letter 8, 1896, page 1, published in *Special Testimonies*, Series A, No. 10, page 25; the phrases "the third person of the Godhead" and "no modified energy" are also used by John Harris in *The Great Teacher*, page 182.

were many biblical subjects that would need further clarification, because the early brethren came from different churches with conflicting opinions and, thus, were not in union on all points of faith.

To expect that she should deal with all biblical subjects at once in full detail would not be reasonable. The early Advent believers were united on the soon coming of Christ but differed in their understanding of various other points of biblical teaching. At first, they did not keep the Sabbath, they were not clear on the Sanctuary or the Spirit of Prophecy, the nature of man and healthful living. Should we build a case regarding Ellen White's understanding based on the rather limited understanding of the early Adventists on these subjects? This is unreasonable and unnecessary. In due time, God provided more detailed insights on the truth, laying a solid foundation of truth in the early days, block by block.

It should not surprise us that Ellen White did not present all points of truth from the very beginning. Yet, this should not be interpreted as her having or presenting incorrect views, for that would be unfair and unreasonable. Looking at the facts, we see that subject after subject was made clear to her, but not all at once. Ellen White would only be blamable if she wrote and proclaimed something that were untrue or heretical. Yet, that is clearly not the case. We can confidently say that what she presented was always true, solid, and biblical, even though her earlier statements were not always as detailed or complete as her later ones.

Consider the following testimony Ellen White's, written in 1904: "Many of our people do not realize how firmly

Ellen White and the Holy Spirit

the foundation of our faith has been laid ..." Brethren, "who were keen, noble, and true, were among those who, after the passing of the time in 1844, searched for truth as for hidden treasure...." (*Selected Messages*, vol. 1, p. 206). At this time, when the believers could not discern the truth, the Spirit of the Lord would come upon Ellen White, and she would be taken off in vision, and a clear explanation would be given her. "Thus light was given that helped us to understand the scriptures in regard to Christ, His mission, and His priesthood. A *line of truth extending from that time to the time when we shall enter the city of God*, was made plain to me and I gave to others the instruction that the Lord had given me" (*Selected Messages*, vol. 1, p. 206, emphasis supplied).

Thus, from the beginning, a firm foundation was laid, and a continuous "line of truth" extended to Christ's coming. No wonder Ellen White encouraged all to hold fast the original truths: "If you *continue to believe and obey the truths you first embraced regarding the personality of the Father and the Son*, you will be joined together with him in love" (*Review and Herald*, March 8, 1906, emphasis supplied).[13] There is no need to

---

13. She had repeated this same teaching about the personhood of the Father in 1891: "The Lord Jesus came to our world to represent the Father. He represented God not as an essence that pervaded nature, but as a God who has a personality. Christ was the express image of His Father's person; and He came to our world to restore in man God's moral image, in order that man, although fallen, might through obedience to God's commandments become enstamped with the divine image and character—adorned with the beauty of divine loveliness" (manuscript dated "about 1891," in *Manuscript Releases*, vol. 19, p. 250).

entertain doubts regarding Ellen White's understanding in her early ministry.

Since Ellen White says that a solid foundation was laid in the early years and encouraged believers to maintain the original truths, would it not be proper to consider how this counsel relates to her supposed maturation in understanding on the Trinity over the years? Does this assertion fit the facts? Is it possible that what some consider to be a more mature view is in reality a deviation from the original platform of truth? We should be careful not to make unwarranted assertions, for a firm foundation has been laid; God has given a "line of truth," which did not begin with faulty or immature views.

Over the years, the Holy Spirit inspired Ellen White to produce statements of greater detail concerning the Trinity. In 1888, it was time for "righteousness by faith" and "Christ our Righteousness" to come more explicitly to the front. At the same time, Christ's oneness and equality with the Father was more powerfully emphasized. "For in him dwelleth all the fulness of the Godhead bodily" (Col. 2:9). "All the fullness" dwells in Him. This means that there is nothing of the Godhead that does not dwell in Him and that He is, therefore, fully divine. God used E. J. Waggoner to accomplish both objectives.

Waggoner taught that Christ, as the Son of the self-existent God, possesses by nature all the attributes of Divinity. Waggoner recognized that, in Psalm 45:6, 7, God the Father is the speaker and that He is addressing the Son as "O God" (see application in Heb. 1:8).

Waggoner also presented Christ as part of the Godhead, and he used the word "Godhead" in the sense of the Trinity or Triune God. He wrote:

> Only a transcendent Christ, who is completely and intrinsically One of the constituent Persons of the ETERNAL GODHEAD in the highest and fullest sense, could be our all-sufficient Creator, Lawgiver, Atoning Sacrifice, Redeemer, Judge, Advocate, Justifier, Sanctifier, Glorifier, and Coming King. Only such a One could constitute the sole and completely adequate Source of the Righteousness imperative for sinful man to stand fully transformed and panoplied in the presence of God's immaculate holiness. (*Christ and His Righteousness*, p. 43)

Ellen White clearly endorsed the 1888 message of Righteousness by Faith in all its fullness through Christ in all His fullness, and she declared soon after, that Waggoner's presentation about the "matchless charms of Christ" was "the first clear teaching on this subject from any human lips I had heard, excepting the conversations between myself and my husband." She testified that she recognized its heavenly origin clearly because "God has presented it to me in vision," and she declared impressively, "When another [she means Waggoner] presented it, every fiber of my heart said, Amen" (Ms. 5, 1889, in *Manuscript Releases*, vol. 5, p. 219).

In 1869, Ellen White had written that Christ, as our Saviour, "possessed divine majesty, perfection, and excellence. He was equal with God" (*Testimonies*, vol. 2, p. 200). Ellen White's husband, James, wrote in 1877 a clear and powerful article on the position of Christ, entitled: "Christ Equal with God," in which he denounced the Unitarian view as erroneous that "makes Christ inferior to the Father" (James White, *Review and Herald*, Nov. 29, 1877, p. 172).[14]

Consequently, Ellen White was not ignorant about the true position and mission of Christ, nor is there evidence that she held wrong views about the Holy Spirit. Since it was essential that God's church accept the 1888 message, Ellen White was inspired to stress its importance as well as Christ's position, the role of the Holy Spirit, and the Triune nature of the Godhead.

---

14. His statement is: "The inexplicable trinity that makes the godhead three in one and one in three, is bad enough; but that ultra Unitarianism that makes Christ inferior to the Father is worse. Did God say to an inferior, 'Let us make man in our image?' " (James White, *Review and Herald*, Nov. 29, 1877, p. 172).

Chapter 3

DID ELLEN WHITE REVERSE HER BELIEF?

Some take certain statements of Ellen White in support of their claim that she believed for a time that Deity could die and that she changed that position in 1904, when she plainly stated that Deity could *not* die. Following are the pertinent statements involved in these claims:

QUOTATION NUMBER 1

What Christ Risked

Remember that Christ risked all; "tempted like as we are," he staked even his own eternal existence upon the issue of the conflict. Heaven itself was imperiled for our redemption. (*General Conference Bulletin,* Dec. 1895, p. 639; cf. *Christ's Object Lessons,* p. 196)

Does this statement actually assert that Deity could die? Existence and divine nature are not one and the same. Is it proper to interpret Mrs. White's statement as asserting that, if Christ had failed in His mission, Deity would have died and ceased to be—that is, that there would be no Father, no Son, and no Holy Spirit? Is that the implication of Ellen White's statement?

What she actually said is that Christ "staked even his own eternal existence upon the issue of the conflict." This means that, in becoming man, Christ did not cling to His eternal, glorious existence, but was willing to lay it aside. Nonetheless, Ellen White's accusers see in these words a clear statement about the potential of Christ's divinity dying. We can speculate about what would have happened had Jesus failed to redeem man and in what sense His eternal existence was at stake, but God has not revealed what actually could have happened. When we contemplate this subject, we should do so with awe and reverence. Christ's nature and work are mysteries that will never be fully understood. Ellen White wrote:

> The most gifted men on earth could all find abundant employment, from now until the judgment, for all their God-given powers in exalting the character of Christ. But they would still fail to present Him as He is. The mysteries of redemption, embracing Christ's divine-human character, His incarnation, His atonement for sin, could employ the pens and the highest mental powers of the wisest men from now until Christ should be revealed in

the clouds of heaven in power and great glory. But though these men should seek with all their power to give a representation of Christ and His work, the representation would fall far short of the reality. (Letter 280, 1904, in *Lift Him Up*, p. 76)

The truth is that we do not know everything about Christ and His work or what would have happened had Christ failed in His mission. If Christ could have failed in His humanity, would that mean that He would have also failed in His divinity? Whatever our imagination tells us on this, it falls "far short of the reality."

To redeem fallen man, Christ could not retain His divine glory and eternal existence. He had to step down and take the form and nature of a man. He laid aside His divinity. Yet, this does not at all mean that He *renounced* or *disclaimed* His divinity. Ellen White wrote: "… Jesus, the Son of God, the world's Redeemer, laid aside His divinity, and came to earth in the garb of humanity" (*Bible Echo*, Oct. 12, 1896). To be our Saviour, Christ needed to be truly God and truly man. With His divine arm, He could grasp the throne of God; with His human arm, He could encircle the fallen human race (*Signs of the Times*, Jan. 24, 1878).

If Christ had failed in His mission of redemption, then Satan would have become the great conqueror. What impression would that have made upon the angels and the unfallen beings of the universe? Would their trust in Christ be affirmed, or would it be shocked and shattered? Was this what she meant when she said: "Heaven itself was imperiled for our redemption" or when she said: "He staked even His own eternal existence"? If that were true, Christ's failure would then have always been carried upon His divine eternal existence?

If Christ had failed in His human nature, does that mean that He would have had to suffer eternal death in His divine nature? Note what Ellen White wrote in her 1888 book about Lucifer's early rebellion: "Though he had forsaken his position as covering cherub, yet if he had been willing to return to God, acknowledging the Creator's wisdom, and satisfied to fill the place appointed him in God's great plan, he would have been reinstated in his office" (*The Great Controversy*, p. 495). If this applied to a rebellious, high-ranking leader next to Christ, would there not also have been a reinstatement somehow for Christ had He failed in His human nature in redeeming fallen human beings?

Yet, since Christ is equal with His Father and superior to Satan, there may have been a difference in consequences. Note Ellen White's words, written in 1893: "The new tomb enclosed Him in its rocky chambers. If one single sin had tainted His character the stone would never have been rolled away from the door of His rocky chamber, and the world with its burden of guilt would have perished" (Diary, July 2, 1893, in *Manuscript Releases*, vol. 10, p. 385). In 1898, she wrote:

> Could Satan in the least particular have tempted Christ to sin, he would have bruised the Saviour's head. As it was, he could only touch His heel. Had the head of Christ been touched, the hope of the

human race would have perished. Divine wrath would have come upon Christ as it came upon Adam. Christ and the church would have been without hope. (*Signs of the Times*, June 9, 1898, in *Selected Messages*, bk. 1, p. 256)

How are we to understand this statement? If Christ had sinned in His human nature, would He too have been without hope in His divine nature? What exactly would have happened to His deity in relation to the other members of the Godhead?

We do not fully understand Christ's redemptive work or what consequences a failure in that work would have had on the Trinity and Godhead. Nonetheless, had Christ failed, the 1898 statement that affirms that Satan "could only touch His heel" makes perfectly clear that the early statement about his staking "even his own eternal existence upon the issue of the conflict," is not the equivalent of saying that His divinity was capable of dying.

QUOTATION NUMBER 2

Deity Could Not Be Lost While Christ Stood Faithful

A second statement, written in 1899, is taken as evidence that Ellen White once believed that Deity could die:

> Though Christ humbled Himself to become man, *the Godhead* was still His own. His Deity could not be lost while He stood faithful and true to His loyalty. (*Signs of the Times,* May 10, 1899)

Did Ellen White Reverse Her Belief? 61

Does Ellen White really say here that Deity could die? She says: "His Deity could not be lost while He stood faithful...." By this does she mean that His deity could have died? Are the loss of Deity and the death of Deity equivalent? No, losing and dying are two different things.

If we think this passage over, we can understand what it means. As long as Christ remained completely loyal, He could not lose His deity. Thus, if Christ, in any way, would become unfaithful, untrue and disloyal, He would have lost His deity because such an attitude is incompatible with perfect Deity. It would have been a blatant misrepresentation of the divine nature. In such a position of unfaithfulness and disloyalty, Christ would have ceased to reflect Deity and, therefore, would have lost His deity.

In a similar way, Ellen White explained: "Christ came to our world because He saw that men had lost the image and nature of God" (*Youth Instructor*, Sept. 9, 1897). Men lost the image and nature of God when they became disobedient and ceased to stand faithful and true.

Also, when Satan became disloyal and unfaithful, he lost his high and holy position. Ellen White wrote:

> Once Satan was in co-partnership with God, Jesus Christ, and the holy angels. He was highly exalted in heaven and was radiant in light and glory that came to him from the Father and the Son, but he became disloyal and lost his high and holy position as covering cherub. (Ms. 39, 1894, in *Christ Triumphant,* p. 10; see John 17:22 regarding the glory given Him by the Father)

Thus, apparently, the same would have applied to Christ had He been unfaithful. He would have lost His deity, but to say that Deity would then have died, is a misuse of Ellen White's words, because that is not what she said.

QUOTATION NUMBER 3

Endangerment of Christ's Divine Attributes

A third passage, written in 1900, is also quoted to substantiate the suggestion that Ellen White believed that Deity could die:

> He became subject to temptation, endangering as it were, His divine attributes. Satan sought, by the constant and curious devices of his cunning, to make Christ yield to temptation. (Letter 5, 1900, in the *Seventh-day Adventist Bible Commentary*, vol. 7, p. 926)

This statement makes clear that Christ had to deal with severe temptations. Satan did his utmost to deceive Christ and get Him to yield to his temptations. In that way, His divine attributes were endangered. Would that mean that Deity would have died had Christ failed by yielding to Satan's temptations?

Note that the word "Deity" is not mentioned in the above statement. We only read that His divine attributes were endangered. Is that the same as saying that Deity would have died? Are all divine attributes an inherent part of Deity? Not all divine attributes are characteristic or typical of Deity. The angels of God reflect God's nature, and they reveal divine character attributes, even as Adam did when he was created in God's image and nature. This does not mean that either the angels or man, in their innocent state, shared Deity. Moreover, although we believe in the deity of Christ, we cannot say that all divine attributes are synonymous with Deity. Therefore, if Christ's divine attributes are at risk, does this necessitate that Ellen White meant that Deity could die? We should be careful with such conclusions. Ellen White warned in 1888: "We must not measure God or His truth by our finite understanding or by our preconceived opinions" (morning talk, Oct. 18, 1888, in *Review and Herald*, Oct. 8, 1889, p. 625). Human reasoning is insufficient to explain God's nature.

There is no greater truth in Scripture than that Jesus died for humankind (1 Thess. 4:14; 2 Cor. 5:15; 1 Tim. 1:15). Yet, on Calvary's cross, it was only the humanity of Christ that died. The divine personhood of the second member of the Trinity could not die. Thus, only a human sacrifice was made at Calvary. The divine Christ did not die but raised His own humanity from the tomb. Christ testified that He had power to lay down His life and power to take it up again, and He added that He had received this command of His Father (John 10:17, 18). Yet, it is also said that the Father raised the Son to life (Acts 13:33, 34, 37). Thus, the Father and the Son worked together in full accord. Christ, who had submitted all to His Father, took up His life by the Father's authority and command.

There are some, however, who believe that Christ also made a *divine* sacrifice. They stress that God and Christ are two distinct divine beings, each possessing the same kind of divine nature. They picture a fully divine sacrifice on Calvary in that the divine Person of Christ, in whom the two natures were "mysteriously blended," laid down both His human and His divine life.[15] Thus, they are not particularly surprised to hear that the divine nature could die.

They explain that the Father's Deity could not die, for the death of Him, in whom all nature exists, would mean the extinction of the entire universe. That is why they propose that, the Father, in His great love, brought forth a Son from Himself as "a part of Himself" (Letter 36a, 1890, in *Our High Calling*, p. 12), that His Son might die the second death—total separation from God—taking with Him in

---

15. The phrase "mysteriously blended" appeared in two of Ellen White's letters—Letter 280 (Sept. 3), 1904 and Letter 8a (July 7), 1890, in *Manuscript Releases*, vol. 6, page 112. Among other works, the phrase appears also in Joseph Henry Allen, *Ten Discourses on Orthodoxy*, pages 70, 71, and John Philip, *Rays of Light: or, Church-Themes and Life-Problems*, pages 241, 242.

that eternal death the sins of mankind. However, they reason, because Christ committed no sin Himself, His Father raised Him up again from the dead. Although the idea of producing an expendable divine being may seem plausible and useful, we can be sure that divinity did not actually die.

QUOTATION NUMBER 4

The Impossibility of Deity Dying

Around 1904, however, Ellen White is supposed to have become quite clear on the issue of the mortality of Deity, when, as some assert, she had reversed her belief and come to understand that Deity could *not* die:

> Was the human nature of the Son of Mary changed into the divine nature of the Son of God? No; the two natures were mysteriously blended in one person—the man Christ Jesus. In Him dwelt all the fullness of the Godhead bodily. When Christ was crucified, it was His human nature that died. Deity did not sink and die; that would have been impossible. (Letter 280, 1904, in *Seventh-day Adventist Bible Commentary*, vol. 5, p. 1113).[16]

---

16. Similar words are used by Heman Humphrey in *The Great Teacher*, page xv: "And *was the human nature of the son of Mary changed into the divine nature?* No—but *the two were mysteriously* united, so as to become *one person.* '*The man Christ Jesus,*' was not 'the Lord from heaven;' but '*in him dwelt all the fullness of the Godhead bodily.*' The *Deity did not* suffer and *sink* under the agonies of Calvary, and yet in the person of Jesus, God there purchased the church with his own blood. A great mystery, but no absurdity" (the italicized words are also used by Humphrey).

This statement is supposed to mark Ellen White's reversal of belief into Trinitarianism and the idea that Deity could *not* die. This could only be true if Ellen White had stated before 1904 that Deity *could* die and directly contradicted the doctrine of the Trinity. However, neither is the case. Ellen White did not leave any statement that directly contradicts the Trinity, nor did she make any statement about Deity being able to die. One can only sustain the opposite conclusion by artificially interjecting preconceived notions into the text.

Quotation Number 5

Deity Did Not Die

The following statement also says very clearly that Deity did *not* die:

> When the voice of the angel was heard saying, "Thy Father calls thee," He who had said, "I lay down my life, that I might take it again," "Destroy this temple, and in three days I will raise it up," came forth from the grave to life that was in Himself. Deity did not die. Humanity died, but Christ now proclaims over the rent sepulcher of Joseph, "I am the Resurrection, and the Life." In His divinity Christ possessed the power to break the bonds of death. He declares that He had life in Himself to quicken whom He will. (Ms. 131, 1897 in *Seventh-day Adventist Bible Commentary*, vol. 5, p. 1113)[17]

---

17. The statement, "Thy Father calls thee," though not found in Scripture, is consistent with the nearly thirty recorded instances of the Father raising His Son from the dead (Acts 2:24, 32; 3:15, 26; 4:10; 5:30; 10:40; 13:30, 34, 37; 17:31; Rom. 4:24; 6:4; 10:9; 1 Cor. 6:14; 15:15; 2 Cor. 4:14; Gal. 1:1; Eph. 1:19, 20; Col. 2:12; 1 Thess. 1:9, 10; 1 Peter 1:21). "He was in that stony prison house as a prisoner of divine justice. He was responsible to the Judge of the universe. He was bearing the sins of the world, and His Father only could release Him" (Ms. 94, 1897 in *Seventh-day Adventist Bible Commentary*, vol. 5, p. 1114). Jesus' statement in John 10:18 ends with: "This commandment have I received of my Father." Only by the Father's authority and command could Christ take up His life again (cf. John 5:30; 8:28). Two other descriptions attribute His renewed life to the Spirit (Rom. 8:11; 1 Peter 3:18).

Some argue that the year 1904 was a great turning point in Ellen White's thinking, for they suppose that this was when she came to understand and believe that Deity could not die. This reversal they see as a victory she gained in obtaining a clearer picture of God's nature. They assert that she left her earlier immature concepts behind at this time, and experienced an epiphany, as the Scriptures opened her eyes to greater understanding.

Though these words may sound possible, do they really present a summary of the facts? Or should we regard these words as artificial and presumptuous? Was the year 1904 indeed a great turning point in Ellen White's thinking? Was it when she came to understand that Deity could not die? Was there a gradual maturation in Ellen White's understanding on this point?

Note that Ellen White did not write the statement about it not being possible for Deity to die in 1904, but several years before that—in 1897. This indicates that, before 1904, Ellen White did *not* believe that Deity could die. She did *not* reverse her view in 1904, but held the view that Deity could not die for at least seven years before this.[18] Nonetheless, another powerful statement goes back even further.

---

18. This is a strong point demonstrating Ellen White's doctrinal consistency. Other examples are: "the lovely Jesus that He is a person.... His Father was a person and had a form like Himself" (*A Sketch of the Christian Experience and Views of Ellen G. White*, p. 64) and "There is a personal God, the Father; there is a personal Christ, the Son" (Ms. 86, 1898, in *Manuscript Releases*, vol. 3, p. 347). Her view is in harmony with the teaching of Scripture, when Paul wrote: "There is but one God, the Father ... and one Lord Jesus Christ" (1 Cor. 8:6).

QUOTATION NUMBER 6

Christ's Divinity Ever Withstanding Death

The following quotation, written ten years before the previous, clearly portrays Christ's deity and the immortality of His divine nature.

> He voluntarily assumed human nature. It was his own act, and by his own consent. He clothed his divinity with humanity. He was all the while as God, but he did not appear as God. He veiled the demonstrations of Deity which had commanded the homage, and called forth the admiration, of the universe of God.... He was God, but the glories of the form of God he for a while relinquished.... As a member of the human family he was mortal; but as a God, he was the fountain of life to the world. He could, in his divine person, ever have withstood the advances of death, and refused to come under its dominion. (*Review and Herald*, July 5, 1887)[19]

This statement illustrates the deity of Christ, as well as the fact that He was only mortal in His human nature and not in His divine nature, which again demonstrates that Deity could not die.

Thus, it is not true that she reversed her belief on this matter in 1904, as if she needed the Scriptures to give her a theological epiphany. None of the three quotations of 1895, 1899, or 1900, supports the suggestion that Ellen White believed that Deity could die, for in 1887 and again in 1897, she clearly stated that Deity could *not* die. The assertion that Ellen White supposedly reversed her belief on this point in 1904 and ever after believed that Deity could not die is, therefore, completely unfounded.

---

19. It is interesting to note that Anglican cleric Henry Melvill used similar expressions in a sermon: "... *He was* still *God*, and could not, for a lonely instant, cease to be God. *But he did not appear as God.* He put from him, or *he veiled*, those effulgent *demonstrations of Deity which had commanded the homage, and called forth the admiration of* the celestial hierarchy. And though *he was, all the while, God*, God *as* truly, and *as* actually, as when, in the might of manifested Omnipotence, he filled infinite space with glorious masses of architecture, still he so restrained the blazings of Divinity that he could not, in the same sense, be known as God, but wanted the form whilst retaining the essence.... As mere man, *he was mortal. But* then as *God, the* well-spring *of life to the* population of the universe, he could forever *have withstood the advances of death, and* have *refused* its *dominion* in his own divine person" (*Sermons*, vol. 1, pp. 43, 48, italicized words used in *Review and Herald*, July 5, 1887)

"As a God" is an interesting choice of words. It refers to Jesus' being divine. Ellen White's usage of the phrase is consistent with her understanding of the Father and the Son as two distinct personal beings. "He was God" describes who Christ was in infinity past. It is what He is by nature, but not in personhood, for the Father and Son are separate divine beings. Christ was not "the God" but "a God," for He was "a part of God Himself."

Chapter 4

ELLEN WHITE'S DESCRIPTION OF GOD

Ellen White, in her supposed semi-Arian view, described God as having body parts and passion. She did emphasize that man was to bear God's image, both in outward resemblance and in character. It is on that basis that some conclude that, in Ellen White's mind, God had the outward appearance of a man, complete with body parts and passion. The following are statements Ellen White wrote on this subject:

STATEMENT 1

Christ Alone – "The Express Image" of the Father

Man was to bear God's image, both in outward resemblance and in character. Christ alone is "the express image" (Hebrews 1:3) of the Father; but man was formed in the likeness of God. (*Patriarchs and Prophets*, p. 45)

We should realize that we are on holy ground when we try to describe God's physical nature. It is presumptuous and dangerous to assert that God has no body parts or passion. How can we know that? Has God revealed that to us? Note again Ellen White's warning: "We must not measure God or His truth by our finite understanding or by our preconceived opinions" (*Review and Herald*, Oct. 8, 1889, from a talk given Oct. 18, 1888). We cannot explain God with our finite human mind. In dealing with the Godhead, we should be filled with awe, reverence and faith.

Most are familiar with the story of Uzzah, the man who touched the ark of the covenant and fell dead (2 Sam. 6:6, 7). Though the ark was holy, its holiness was only a dim reflection of the holiness of God. What then should we expect, if we touch the holy God with our limited finite minds trying to describe Him?

How foolish it is to go beyond that which God in His infinite wisdom has revealed. Satan delights to have humans try to figure God out. While there are urgent subjects to study in this time of the end, regarding God's existence and nature, only humble trust is appropriate.

It is puzzling how a sinful, finite human being would attempt to describe our all-wise holy and infinite God.[20] Simply to come into His presence would cause immediate death, for God is a consuming fire. It is insolent boldness

---

20. It is not essential for us to define what God is, but only to know who He and Jesus Christ are—"And this is life eternal, that they might know thee the only true God, and Jesus Christ whom thou has sent" (John 17:3).

Ellen White's Description of God

to claim that He has neither body parts nor passion, for that is not what the Bible indicates.

We cannot measure God with earthly things. Man is fallen and has become finite and mortal. Man was created perfect, having a glorious body "with a covering of light and glory, such as the angels wear" (*Patriarchs and Prophets*, p. 45; *Signs of the Times*, Jan. 9, 1879). That glorious covering of light is gone, which covered the glorious body made in the likeness of God. Now we see but a reflection of the outward resemblance of God's image. Just how glorious was the human body when God originally created it? We simply do not know, but it must have been very wonderful and unutterably brilliant, since man delighted to be in God's presence! Not being able to imagine man's original glory in our current fallen state, it does not make sense to discuss how man would have originally reflected the outward resemblance of God's image.

Ellen White's supposed view of God having the "form and feature" of a man is also seen in the following statement:

STATEMENT 2

The Likeness of God Includes Form and Feature

> In the beginning, man was created in the likeness of God, not only in character, but in form and feature. (*Spirit of Prophecy*, vol. 4, p. 463)

If we read this statement in its context, as presented in *The Great Controversy*, we will understand this sentence better, and we will not find any semi-Arianism in Ellen White's view of the sleeping saints' coming forth from their graves:

> Adam, who stands among the risen throng, is of lofty height and majestic form, in stature but little below the Son of God. He presents a marked contrast to the people of later generations; in this one respect is shown the great degeneracy of the race.... In the beginning, man was created in the likeness of God, not only in character, but in form and feature. Sin defaced and almost obliterated the divine image; but Christ came to restore that which had been lost. He will change our vile bodies, and fashion them like unto His glorious body. The mortal, corruptible form, devoid of comeliness, once polluted with sin, becomes perfect, beautiful, and immortal. All blemishes and deformities are left in

the grave. Restored to the tree of life in the long-lost Eden, the redeemed will "grow up" (Malachi 4:2) to the full stature of the race in its primeval glory. The last lingering traces of the curse of sin will be removed, and Christ's faithful ones will appear in "the beauty of the Lord our God;" in mind and soul and body reflecting the perfect image of their Lord. (*The Great Controversy*, pp. 644, 645)

The things of this sinful world cannot describe God. No wonder the prophet asks: "To whom then will ye liken God? or what likeness will ye compare unto him?" (Isaiah 40:18). Although the prophet asks this question in the context of false gods worshipped through graven images, it is certainly true that there is nothing on this fallen, sinful planet that compares to God's glorious outward appearance.

The original primeval glory of man has been lost. Adam was of majestic form, in great contrast with later generations, due to the great degeneracy of the race. Sin defaced and almost obliterated the divine image. There is no way to compare God with the current "form and feature" of man.

But Christ came to restore our bodies like unto His glorious body, and, when we are restored to the tree of life, we will *grow up* to the full primeval glory.

Thus, even when we are saved in God's Kingdom, we will still have a way to go in reaching the full original glory. Only that original, gloriously blessed state of man is in the least comparable to the likeness of God's being.

In that context, we read about Christ's joy and glory with the redeemed, at the close of the thousand years. Then, "He looks upon the redeemed, renewed in his own image, every heart bearing the perfect impress of the divine, every face reflecting the likeness of their King" (*The Great Controversy,* p. 671).

We will not truly reflect God's likeness in form and outward resemblance until we are glorified and renewed in God's eternal Kingdom. Says the apostle John: "… when he shall appear, we shall be like him; for we shall see him as he is" (1 John 3:2).

As compared with man in his original, sinless state, the Bible and Ellen White clearly picture God as having body parts. This includes arms, hands and feet, ears and eyes and a mouth. It also includes His having passion and feelings, such as love and sympathy towards those who walk uprightly and feelings of antipathy and anger towards those who rebelliously live in sin, despising His saving grace and love.

The Bible and Ellen White call attention to what will be the only remaining trace of humanity's experience with sin:

> One reminder alone remains: our Redeemer will ever bear the marks of His crucifixion. Upon His wounded head, upon His side, His hands and feet, are the only traces of the cruel work that sin has wrought. Says the prophet, beholding Christ in His glory, "He had bright beams coming out of His side: and there was the hiding of His power." Habakkuk 3:4, margin. That pierced side whence flowed the crimson stream that reconciled man to God—there is the Saviour's glory, there "the hiding of His power." … And the tokens of His humiliation are His highest honor; through the eternal ages the wounds of Calvary

will show forth His praise and declare His power" (*The Great Controversy*, p. 674).

If God has seen fit to describe Himself with body parts in His holy Word, why should we not accept the testimony of Scripture and seek to better understand it?

Chapter 5

ELLEN WHITE, A TRINITARIAN

Some believe that a statement of Ellen White's husband, James, provides strong evidence that his wife did not believe in the Trinity in 1871. James certainly knew his wife better than anyone else did, and he must have known what she believed. Here is his testimony:

> We invite all to compare the testimonies of the Holy Spirit through Mrs. W., with the word of God. And in this we do not invite you to compare them with your creed. That is quite another thing. The trinitarian may compare them with his creed, and because they do not agree with it, condemn them. The observer of Sunday, or the man who holds eternal torment an important truth, and the minister that sprinkles infants, may each condemn the testimonies of Mrs. W. because they do not agree with their peculiar views. And a hundred more, each holding different views, may come to the same conclusion. But their genuineness can

never be tested in this way. (James White, *Review and Herald*, June 13, 1871, p. 204)

Some surmise from this statement that, if Ellen White had been a Trinitarian, her husband would not have put "the trinitarian ... with his creed" in opposition to "Mrs. W." Thus, they conclude, she must not have been a Trinitarian in her early ministry. James White's statement is regarded as convincing evidence that should end all controversy on this point.

Considering this statement, we might wonder: Did James White really say here that his wife was not a Trinitarian or that she was a semi-Arian? Can we find in Ellen White's writings any statement that is out of harmony with the concept of the Trinity? Is there any clear evidence that Ellen White was not a Trinitarian in her early ministry? Those who think so build their case on suppositions that are doubtful and unsound.

From a careful reading of what James White said about Trinitarianism, it is clear that he did not say that his wife did not believe in the Trinity. No, he invites all to compare the Spirit's testimonies through his wife with the Bible and not with any creed. That, certainly, is a good attitude for no creed can take the place of the Bible. Then he says: "The trinitarian may compare them with his creed, and because they do not agree with it, condemn them." Apparently, the trinitarian creed that James White had in mind was one that was out of harmony with Scripture and his wife's testimonies.

A further relevant question is: What kind of Trinitarian creed could be intended here by James White? Many, in that era, accepted the description of the Trinity in the first article of faith in the Methodist Creed:

> **Article I.—Of Faith in the Holy Trinity.**
> There is but one living and true God, everlasting, without body or parts, of infinite power, wisdom, and goodness; the maker and preserver of all things, both visible and invisible. And in unity of this Godhead there are three persons, of one substance, power, and eternity—the Father, the Son, and the Holy Ghost. (*The Book of Discipline of the United Methodist Church*, p. 61)

A bibliographical note on the previous page says: "The Articles of Religion are here reprinted from the Discipline of 1808." This would tend to validate this being the creed that James and Ellen White believed was in contradiction of the Scriptures.[21]

If we consider the stipulations of this article of the Methodist faith, we can understand why James White invited all to compare the testimonies of the Holy Spirit through his wife with the Word of God, because there is certainly something in this article of Methodist faith that is out of harmony with the Bible and Ellen White's testimonies.

The phrase "God, everlasting, without body or parts" does not only clash with the Bible, but it also clashes with the teachings in Ellen White's writings. There are many

---

21. Another support for this being the creed James White meant is that this same article of faith was quoted by J. B. Frisbie in a discussion of the doctrine of the Trinity in *Review and Herald*, March 7, 1854, page 50.

places in the Bible where God is described as having body parts, and Ellen White has testified many times, including in her early writings, that God is not without body or parts. This, evidently, was among a number of people quite an issue, and many were inclined to spiritualize God as well as Christ's coming. This is why Ellen White asked Jesus in vision whether His Father was also a person and had the same form as Jesus (*Early Writings*, pp. 54, 77).

As to several articles of faith, quite a few people, judging by their creed, made this a criterion to judge the reliability of Ellen White's testimonies. It is no wonder that James urged all not to compare Ellen's testimonies with their creed, but with the Bible. That is the way to handle Ellen White's writings. Creeds, articles and principles of faith should all be compared with the Bible.

If we insist that Ellen White did not believe in the Trinity in 1871, we miss the point, for it is not the sound, biblical Trinity that is at stake in James White's statement, but rather the *kind* of Trinity that was believed to be true by many but which is not in full harmony with the teachings of the Scriptures.

Thus, it should be clear that James White's statement does not provide convincing evidence that Ellen White, in her early ministry, was a semi-Arian and not a Trinitarian. There is also no indication that she held on to the Methodist Trinitarian creed, during her life, as some assert.

Several clear statements indicate that Ellen White certainly was a Trinitarian. Some hold, nevertheless, that she became, as late as 1890 or 1893, a Trinitarian. Others insist that it was around 1897. Whichever way, there is no solid evidence for such an inference. If there were, would that not raise doubts as to when she was fully inspired? Moreover, would there then not be a period of transition, which would blur the boundaries of being less or fully inspired? Is this truly the way God inspires the work of His servants?

It is true that Ellen White was rather silent in her early ministry about the nature of the Trinity, but that does not prove she did not believe in the doctrine.

Some twenty-eight years before her supposed epiphany, she stated in Testimonies, No. 17 (1869) that Christ is equal with God, possessing full divine qualities. Furthermore, in 1872, she indicated that, unlike the angels, Christ was not created but is God's divine Son, *equal with God* and, as such, the only sufficient sacrifice to rescue man. She wrote: "The salvation of fallen man was procured at such an immense cost that angels marveled, and could not fully comprehend the divine mystery that the majesty of Heaven, *equal with God*, should die for the rebellious race" (*Review and Herald*, Dec 17, 1872, emphasis supplied). This declaration rules out Arianism and it is in accordance with Trinitarianism. However, back in 1861, she had already written a short statement, consistent with Trinitarianism, regarding the divinity of Christ and His union with the Father. "The world understood not his union with the Father; and the excellency and glory of his divine character were hid from them" (*Review and Herald*, June 25, 1861).

It is true that the pioneers of the Advent movement

were not united in their views of the nature of the Godhead and that they held divergent views on other important biblical teachings.[22] Some did indeed hold semi-Arian views in response to the non-physical views of Deity held by other Christians. Yet, in the early days, these differences were not made a test of fellowship, and, in time, they were blessed with more light and greater understanding and came into line with one another on these different subjects.

As the gift of prophecy in ancient times was a blessing in directing God's people (Num. 12:7; 2 Chron. 20:20; Amos 3:7), so were Ellen White's visions and testimonies invaluable to the Advent people in bringing insight, endorsing truth, and fomenting unity within the church.

Certain subjects took precedence in the early Advent movement, but in due time, God provided insights about the Godhead as the subject was given closer consideration. As the subject became a primary topic of study, the Holy Spirit inspired Ellen White to write clearer statements on the subject.

Just because Ellen White was not as specific and detailed on the subject of the Godhead in her early ministry does not mean that she cherished wrong views or

---

22. Although some "rejected the trinity, yet, with equal unanimity they upheld the divinity of Christ" (Russel Holt, "The Doctrine of the Trinity in the Seventh-day Adventist Denomination: Its Rejection and Acceptance," a term paper for Dr. Mervyn Maxwell, 1969, p. 6). Those who upheld Christ's divinity included: Joseph Bates, James White, J. H. Waggoner, R. F. Cottrell, J. N. Loughborough, J. N. Stephenson, Uriah Smith, A. T. Jones, J. N. Andrews, B. L. Whitney, E. J. Waggoner, Washington Morse, D. M. Canright, James Matteson, A. C. Bourdeau, J. B. Frisbie, S. B. Whitney, A. J. Dennis, M. C. Wilcox, and James Edson White.

presented statements out of harmony with the Bible. On the contrary, there is no need to repudiate any of her earlier statements.

The following are clear statements about the Trinity, written by Mrs. White for the benefit of the church.

Christ's Pre-Existence from All Eternity

"In speaking of His pre-existence, Christ carries the mind back through dateless ages. He assures us that there never was a time when He was not in close fellowship with the eternal God" (*The Signs of the Times*, Aug. 29, 1900).[23]

"But while God's Word speaks of the humanity of Christ when upon this earth, it also speaks decidedly regarding his pre-existence. The Word existed as a divine being, even as the eternal Son of God, in union and oneness with His Father" (*Review and Herald*, April 5, 1906).[24]

---

23. It should be noted that there are two individuals spoken of here: Christ and the eternal God. The phrase "dateless ages" means ages that had no time, as we know it, to mark events or duration. Timelessness is a property of eternity. Christ has always remained in constant fellowship with the eternal God.
24. That is, Christ existed as a divine being, as the eternal Son of God, not as the eternal God. As in the previous quotation, "in union" means "in close fellowship." His Father is the eternal "only true God" (John 17:3). A similar statement is: "There is no one who can explain the mystery of the incarnation of Christ. Yet we know that He came to this earth and lived as a man among men. The man Christ Jesus was not the Lord God Almighty, yet Christ and the Father are one" (Ms. 140, 1903, in *Seventh-day Adventist Bible*

Christ One and Equal and of the Same Substance with the Father

"In all the universe there was but one who could, in behalf of man, satisfy its claims. Since the divine law is as sacred as God Himself, only one equal with God could make atonement for its transgression" (*Patriarchs and Prophets*, p. 63).

"... Jesus said, 'I and my Father are one.' The words of Christ were full of deep meaning as he put forth the claim that he and the Father were of one substance, possessing the same attributes" (*The Signs of the Times*, Nov. 27, 1893).[25]

"Yet the Son of God was the acknowledged sovereign of Heaven, one in power and authority with the Father. In all the counsels of God, Christ was a participant, while Lucifer was not permitted thus to enter into the divine purposes." (*The Great Controversy*, p. 495).[26]

Commentary, vol. 5, p. 1129).

25. The phrase "of one substance" is explained as meaning "possessing the same attributes." What the Father possessed, the Son possessed because the Father gave all things to His Son (Matt. 11:27; Luke 10:22). The relationship is similar to "the stone cut out of the mountain without hands" (Dan. 2:45), which is the same age and material as the mountain from which it came.

26. Two participated in these counsels: God the Father and Christ, the Son of God.

"To save the transgressor of God's law, Christ, the one equal with the Father, came to live heaven before men" (*Review and Herald*, Nov. 17, 1891).[27]

"Immeasurable love was expressed when one equal with the Father came to pay the price for the souls of men, and bring to them eternal life" (*Review and Herald*, March 5, 1908).

"Christ was one with the Father, yet when sin entered our world through Adam's transgression, he was willing to step down from the exaltation of One who was equal with God, who dwelt in light unapproachable by humanity, so full of glory that no man could behold his face and live, and submit to insult, mockery, suffering, pain, and death, in order to answer the claims of the immutable law of God, and make a way of escape for the transgressor by his death and righteousness." (*The Youth's Instructor*, Sept. 27, 1894).

"This Saviour was the brightness of His Father's glory and the express image of His person. He possessed divine majesty, perfection, and excellence. He was equal with God" (*Testimonies for the Church,* vol. 2, p. 200, written in 1869).[28]

---

27. The Son of God is "equal with God," meaning His Father (John 5:18), as Eve was equal with Adam. Having been taken out of Adam, she was fully human—bone of his bones and flesh of his flesh (Gen. 2:23).
28. He was equal by nature—that which is born of the Spirit is spirit (John 3:6). It is on this basis that He was "made a quickening [life-giving] Spirit" (1 Cor. 15:45).

The Divinity and Personhood of the Holy Spirit

"Sin could be resisted and overcome only through the mighty agency of the Third Person of the Godhead, who would come with no modified energy, but in the fullness of divine power. It is the Spirit that makes effectual what has been wrought out by the world's Redeemer" (*The Desire of Ages*, p. 671).[29]

---

29. Adapted from Letter 8, 1896, page 1, in *Special Testimonies*, Series A, No. 10, page 25, compare with John Harris, *The Great Teacher*, page 182. Two sentences later she says: "*Christ has given His Spirit* as a *divine power* to overcome all hereditary and cultivated tendencies to evil, and to impress *His own character* upon His church" (*The Desire of Ages*, p. 671, emphasis supplied).

What is the only way "sin could be resisted and overcome"? Ellen White answers: "There is *but one power* that can break the hold of evil from the hearts of men, and that is *the power of God in Jesus Christ. Only* through the blood of the Crucified One is there cleansing from sin. *His grace alone* can enable us to *resist and subdue* the tendencies of our fallen nature" (*Testimonies for the Church*, vol. 8, p. 291, written in 1903, emphasis supplied).

"There is *only one power* that can turn the sinner from sin to holiness,— the power of Christ. Our Redeemer is the *only one who can take away sin*" (*Review and Herald*, June 2, 1903, emphasis supplied).

"The *only defense against evil* is the indwelling of *Christ in the heart* through faith in His righteousness" (*The Desire of Ages*, p. 324, emphasis supplied).

"Christ is the source of every right impulse. He is *the only one that can* implant in the heart *enmity against sin*" (*Steps to Christ*, p. 26, emphasis supplied). Therefore, because the Son of man, in whom dwelt the fullness of God, condemned sin in the likeness of sinful flesh, He is *the only agency* through whom sin in our lives can be *resisted* and *overcome*. The Holy Spirit is the "Spirit of Christ" (Rom. 8:9; Phil. 1:19; 1 Peter 1:11).

"The Holy Spirit has a personality, else He could not bear witness to our spirits ... He must also be a divine person, else He could not search out the secrets which lie hidden in the mind of God" (Ms. 20, 1906, in *Manuscript Releases*, vol. 20, p. 69).[30]

---

30. "God has sent the Spirit of His Son" means that the Spirit has personhood and is a divine person. The phrase "search out the secrets hidden in the mind of God" refers to 1 Corinthians 2:10. Jesus said, "No man ... knoweth the Father, save the Son" (Matt. 11:27), for He is "Christ the power of God, and the wisdom of God" (1 Cor. 1:24). Thus, when Christ dwells in us through His Spirit, "we have the mind of Christ" (1 Cor. 2:16). What a wonderful unity!

92 Ellen White & The Trinity

"… we need to realize that the Holy Spirit, who is as much a person as God is a person, is walking through these grounds" (Ms. 66, 1899, in *Manuscript Releases*, vol. 7, p. 299).[31]

---

31. The entire paragraph is: "[Rom. 12:1, 2 quoted.] *The Lord* says this because *He* knows it is for our good. *He* would build a wall around us, to keep us from transgression, so that *His* blessing and love may be bestowed on us in rich measure. This is the reason we have established a school here. *The Lord* instructed us that this was the place in which we should locate, and we have had every reason to think that we are in the right place. We have been brought together as a school, *and we need to realize that the Holy Spirit, who is as much a person as God is a person, is walking through these grounds, unseen by human eyes; that the Lord God is our Keeper and Helper. He hears every word we utter* and *knows every thought of the mind"* (March 25, 1899 sermon, in *Sermons and Talks*, vol. 2, pp. 136, 137; and in *Manuscript Releases*, vol. 7, p. 299, emphasis supplied).

The context reveals that it is the Lord through the Holy Spirit who walks the grounds, as our Keeper and Helper. It is He who hears every word and knows every thought of the mind. He is the only one who can renew our mind and transform us into His image through the overcoming power of His Spirit. Thus, the close co-operation and unity between God, who is a person, and the Holy Spirit, who is as much a person, is clearly demonstrated here.

Nonetheless, notice that *Christ* also walks unseen among us to work with us, to heal and to bless us: "*Christ* walks unseen through our streets. With messages of mercy *He* comes to our homes. With all who are seeking to minister in His name, *He* waits to co-operate. *He is in the midst of us*, to heal and to bless, if we will receive *Him"* (*The Ministry of Healing*, p. 107, emphasis supplied).

"Remember that *Jesus* is beside you wherever you go, noting your actions and listening to your words" (*Youth's Instructor,* Feb. 4, 1897, emphasis supplied).

"The *Lord Jesus* standing by the side of the canvasser, walking with them, is the chief worker" (*The Bible Echo*, Sept. 18, 1899; *Review and Herald,* Nov. 7, 1899, emphasis supplied). Thus, each Person of the Godhead is actively working in close unity to redeem fallen humanity.

All the Fullness of the Godhead in the Father, Son, and Holy Spirit

"The Father is all the fulness of the Godhead bodily, and is invisible to mortal sight."

"The Son is all the fulness of the Godhead manifested. The Word of God declares Him to be 'the express image of His person.' "

"The Comforter that Christ promised to send after He ascended to heaven, is the Spirit in all the fullness of the Godhead, making manifest the power of divine grace to all who receive and believe in Christ as a personal Saviour.... " (*Special Testimonies*, Series B, No. 7, pp. 62, 63, written in 1905).

The Trinity of the Father, the Son and the Holy Spirit

"There are three living persons of the heavenly trio; in the name of these three great powers—the Father, the Son, and the Holy Spirit—those who receive Christ by living faith are baptized ..." (*Special Testimonies*, Series B, No 7. p. 63).

"We are to co-operate with the three highest powers in heaven, —the Father, the Son, and the Holy Ghost,— and these powers will work through us making us workers together with God...." (*Special Testimonies*, Series B, No. 7, p. 51).

"The three powers of the Godhead, the Father, Son, and Holy Spirit, are pledged to be their strength and their efficiency in their new life in Christ Jesus" (*The Australasian Union Conference Record*, Oct. 7, 1907).

"The three powers of the Godhead have pledged their might to carry out the purpose that God had in mind when he gave to the world the unspeakable gift of his Son" (*Review and Herald*, July 18, 1907).

Ellen White, a Trinitarian

These quotations leave no doubt that Ellen White was a true Bible-believing Trinitarian Christian.[32]

Some people find it a little curious that Scripture and Ellen White's writings so often mention the Father and the Son without the Holy Spirit.[33] They argue that the Father and the Son seem to receive more honor than the Holy

---

32. Commenting on the important text of Matthew 28:19, she wrote: "Christ gave his followers a positive promise that after his ascension he would send them *his Spirit.* 'Go ye therefore,' he said, 'and teach all nations, baptizing them in the name of *the Father [a personal God],* and of *the Son [a personal Prince and Saviour],* and of *the Holy Ghost [sent from heaven to represent Christ]:* teaching them to observe all things whatsoever I have commanded you; and, lo, I am with you alway, even unto the end of the world' " (*Review and Herald,* Oct. 26, 1897, brackets in the original, emphasis supplied).

    Though Ellen White only calls attention here to the personhood of the Father and the Son and not to that of the Holy Spirit, it does not mean that she had doubts about the unique personhood of the Holy Spirit. She plainly stated: "The Holy Spirit is the Comforter, in Christ's name. He personifies Christ, yet is a *distinct personality.* We may have the Holy Spirit if we ask for it and make it [a] habit to turn to and trust in God rather than in any finite human agent who may make mistakes" (Ms. 93, 1893, in *Manuscript Releases,* vol. 20, p. 324, emphasis supplied).

    Nonetheless, the Holy Spirit acts, unlike Christ, *apart* from human nature: "The Holy Spirit is Christ's representative, but divested of the personality of humanity, and independent thereof. Cumbered with humanity, Christ could not be in every place personally. Therefore it was for their interest that He should go to the Father, and send the Spirit to be His successor on earth. No one could then have any advantage because of his location or his personal contact with Christ. By the Spirit the Saviour would be accessible to all. In this sense He would be nearer to them than if He had not ascended on high" (*The Desire of Ages,* p. 669; adapted from *Review and Herald,* April 28, 1891, and Letter 119, 1895, in *Manuscript Releases,* vol. 14, p. 23).

33. She does no different than Daniel, who only described seeing the "Ancient of Days" and the "Son of man" (Dan. 7:13). In Revelation, besides "him who sat on the throne" and the "Lamb that was slain," John described "seven spirits" represented by "seven lamps of fire burning before the throne" (Rev. 4:2, 5; 5:6; 14:1).

Spirit, and they are inclined to think that there is no perfect equality, but rather a difference between the three heavenly powers of the Godhead.

We should not forget that, in God's plan of salvation, there is a difference in the roles of the various members of the Godhead. Perhaps we could say that the Holy Spirit has a more inconspicuous role, because He works in the shadow of Christ's accomplished work. "It is the Spirit that makes effectual what has been wrought out by the world's Redeemer" (*The Desire of Ages*, p. 671). This, however, does not mean that the Spirit's role is less important. "The Spirit was to be given as a regenerating agent, and without this the sacrifice of Christ would have been of no avail" (*The Desire of Ages*, p. 671). Thus, the work of the Holy Spirit is, in fact, the same in kind as that of Christ because the Holy Spirit is *Christ's* Spirit, but also the *Father's*, which stresses perfect unity between the three persons of the Godhead.

Though the work of the Holy Spirit may not be as outstanding as the unique role of the Son, it is nevertheless of urgent importance. Thus, to redeem fallen man, we see between the three heavenly powers in the Godhead different roles of close co-operation in perfect unity.

Scripture describes the Holy Spirit as a person, with masculine pronouns, just as it does the Father and the Son. Personal activities are ascribed to Him, such as speaking, hearing and teaching; appointing, directing and guiding; testifying, sanctifying and glorifying (Acts 8:29; 10:19; 13:2. John 14:26; 15:26; 16:8–15; Rom. 15:16). The Holy Spirit has also feelings and can be vexed and grieved; tempted and resisted (Isa. 63:10; Eph. 4:30; Acts 5:9; 7:51). He has creative power and exercises His own will (Job 33:4; Rom. 15:13; 1 Cor. 12:11).

That the Scriptures use personal pronouns in addressing and referring to the Holy Spirit indicates the transparent nature of the personification.[34]

Jesus called the Holy Spirit "another Comforter" and promised: "And I will pray the Father, and He shall give you another Comforter, that he may abide with you for ever ..." (John 14:16). The Greek words for "another

---

34. If not rightly understood, the use of personal pronouns for identification purposes can be misleading in some cases. For example, Jesus spoke of Himself in third person to the woman at Jacob's well when He said, "If thou knewest the gift of God, and who it is that saith to thee, Give me to drink; thou wouldest have asked of him, and he would have given thee living water" (John 4:10). We likely would have said, *You would have asked of Me, and I would have given you.* Yet, this is the manner in which Jesus spoke, and we may trust that He did so on purpose because He wanted the woman to recognize Him as the Messiah. Christ told her divine truths and presented evidence that He knew her life. Therefore, the woman "began to have some conviction of His character. The question arose in her mind, Might not this be the long-looked-for Messiah? She said to Him, 'I know that Messias cometh, which is called Christ ..." (*The Desire of Ages*, p. 190). Jesus had achieved His goal, and now He answered the woman straightforwardly: "I that speak unto thee am He" (John 4:26).

A similar principle applies in Jesus' conversation with Nicodemus, who "did not acknowledge Jesus to be the Messiah. But only a teacher sent from God." Jesus referred to Himself as "the Son of man" and as God's Son (John 3:13–18). Following his conversation with Jesus, Nicodemus "watched His life, and pondered His teachings" and, "when Jesus was lifted up on the cross," he remembered Christ's teaching and "saw in Jesus the world's Redeemer" (*The Desire of Ages*, pp.168, 176, 177). Thus, by personal experience he accepted Jesus as the Messiah, and that had been Christ's intention. Jesus frequently spoke of Himself in the third person with the intent of making those who listened to Him think. Such examples should not diminish the normal use of personal pronouns for identification purposes.

Comforter" are *allon paraklēton*. The word *allon* is significant. It means *another* distinct but equal Comforter like Christ. If the promised Comforter would be different from Christ—that is, not of the same nature—then John would not have used the word *allon* in Greek but *heteron*.

The Greek word *allon* emphasizes similarity, in other words, that which is of the same nature.

> Thus Christ promises to his disciples that He will send, not *heteron*, but *allon, Paraklēton* (John xiv. 16), 'another' Comforter therefore, similar to Himself. The dogmatic force of this *allos* has in controversy with various sects … *pneumatiomachoi* been often urged before now …." (Trench, *Synonyms of the New Testament*, p. 358)

> Note also that the word *another* is *allon*, and not *heteron*, which means *different*. The advocate who is to be sent is not *different* from Christ, but *another* similar to Himself. (Vincent, *Word Studies in the New Testament*, vol. 2, p. 244)

In Galatians 1:6, Paul wondered why the believers had accepted so quickly "another gospel." This other gospel was not identical with the gospel that the apostles had previously preached to them, and, therefore, because it was a different gospel, the Greek word Paul used was not *allon* but *heteron*.

The word *allon* is also used in Matthew 5:39: "… whosoever shall smite thee on thy right cheek, turn to him the *other* also." The right cheek matches the left cheek; there is no real difference between them, therefore *allon* is used and not the word *heteron.*

Christ designates the Holy Spirit as "another Comforter," which implies that He Himself is also a Comforter, or *paraklētos,* which literally means "one called to the side of," and therefore signifies a mediator, intercessor or advocate (1 John 2:1; cf. Rom. 8:26, 27, 34). If the other Comforter to come, which is comparable to Christ, would be somehow different in nature and not divine, then it would be a *heteron paraklēton*—another Comforter *of a different kind.*[35] However, if the promised other Comforter is "another" that is similar to Christ, sharing the same nature, then the word *allon* would best be used. From the use of *allon* instead of *heteron,* we conclude that the Holy Spirit is indeed of the same nature and substance and not different from Christ.[36]

---

35. "Another of the same kind" can also mean "more of the same kind." *Paraklētos* occurs only in two books of the New Testament, both written by John. In John 14:16, 26; 15:26; 16:7, it is translated "Comforter." In 1 John 2:1, it is translated "Advocate."

    We have only one Advocate who is also our Comforter. The "one mediator between God and men, the man Christ Jesus" (1 Tim. 2:5). His Spirit dwelt in the prophets (1 Pet. 1:10, 11), and He dwells in the inner man—or the spirit—of the believer (Eph. 3:16, 17).

36. "That Christ should manifest himself to them, and yet be invisible to the world, was a mystery to them. They could not understand the words of Christ in [their] spiritual sense. They were thinking of the outward, visible manifestation. They could not take in the fact that they could have *the presence of Christ with them,* and yet he be unseen by the world …" (*Signs of the Times,* Nov. 18, 1897, emphasis supplied). The following year she repeated these words and quoted more of the manuscript, "*They did not understand the meaning of a spiritual manifestation*" (*The Southern Review,* Sept. 13, 1898, emphasis supplied).

    She elaborated on the connection between the Father, the Son and the Spirit in a statement in 1892: "The Father has given His Son for us that *through the Son the Holy Spirit might come* to us, and *lead us unto the*

Thus, as Ellen White indicated, the Holy Spirit is as much a person as God is, fully divine and a member of the Godhead.

Father" (*Signs of the Times*, Oct. 3, 1892, emphasis supplied). Jesus said, "... no man cometh unto the Father but by me" (John 14:6).

Chapter 6

CHRIST'S SUBJECTION TO THE FATHER

The Bible teaches that Christ was to be subject to the Father. Why was that? It was because, within God's great plan of salvation, Christ has always been the lesser One as our Mediator. Will His subjection to the Father ever cease?[37] Will the Father always be greater than the Son? If

---

37. With regard to His divine nature, the Son is not a lesser God. In Him dwells all the fullness of the Godhead. He is "the divine Son of God, the personification of the only true God"—His Father. (Ms. 40, 1897, in *Selected Messages*, bk. 3, p. 416; cf. *Review and Herald*, Jan. 30, 1900). He is the express image of His Father's person; to see the Son is to see the Father (John 14:9). The Father is unbegotten; the Son is begotten—that is the only difference. The Father has given to His Son His own name, which is above every name (Phil. 2:9). Therefore, we honor the Son even as we honor the Father (John 5:23) because He is "the Son of the living God" (Matt. 16:16). Contrary to what His enemies charged, Jesus neither broke the Sabbath nor *made* Himself equal with God. He always kept the Sabbath and was *by nature* equal with God (John 5:18).

Equality within the Godhead means an equal measure of power, position, and authority. The suggestion is that, temporarily, in his role as "Son," Christ accepted a lower position, with less authority and power than the One who took the role of "Father."

the Son humbled Himself, becoming subject to the Father to save lost humanity, why would He need to subject Himself again to the Father? Does this point to an inherent difference between the Father and the Son, indicating that they are not perfectly one and equal?

The following scripture has often been quoted to make clear that the Father and the Son are not equal partners in the Godhead.

> Then cometh the end, when he shall have delivered up the kingdom to God, even the Father: when he shall have put down all rule and all authority and power. For he must reign, till he hath put all enemies under his feet. The last enemy that shall be destroyed is death. For he hath put all things under his feet. But when he saith all things are put under him, it is manifest that he is excepted, which did put all things under him. And when all things shall be subdued unto him, then shall the Son also himself be subject unto him that put all things under him, that God may be all in all. (1 Cor. 15:24–28)

Before the foundation of the earth, the divine council agreed that Christ should humble Himself and become man's Redeemer. He took the form and nature of fallen humanity and was subdued to the Father. We could perhaps say that the Father, as it were, took the leading role of Director, while Christ took the role of Executor of the plan of salvation.

Christ occupies an exceptional position. He is the only Mediator (1 Tim. 2:5), and Redeemer. God has given no

Christ's Subjection to the Father

other name to men "whereby we must be saved" (Acts 4:12). As for man's redemption, the name of Christ is really unique and incomparable. It was not the Father's blood that was shed, but Christ's. It was Christ who paid the price and redeemed fallen humanity and regained the dominion of this earth.

Through man's fall, Satan became the prince and ruler of this earth, but through Christ's death, the devil was *dethroned* or *brought to naught* (Heb. 2:14, *Goodspeed* and *American Standard Version*). Referring to this, Christ testified: "Now is the judgment of this world: now shall the prince of this world be cast out ... This he said, signifying what death he should die" (John 12:31, 33). This is confirmed in Revelation 12:9, 11: "Satan ... was cast out ... And they overcame him by the blood of the Lamb."

So, Christ is the only actual redeemer and deliverer. Through His blood and by giving His life, the dominion of this world became His. Right after His death and resurrection, He testified: "All power is given unto me in heaven and in earth" (Matt. 28:18). Christ was now the lawful, legitimate and legal owner of this fallen world. He had paid the full price.

Being fully divine and distinct from the Father, Christ atoned for man's sin with His human life and, as a great Victor, received all power and authority.[38] Being equal and one with the Father, He possessed—like the Father—all power in heaven. However, after having paid the price on the cross of Calvary, He came into possession of all power on earth, because Satan, the prince of this world, was dethroned and brought to naught through His death.

When Christ suffered the penalty of sin, the angels "suffered with Christ," their leader, and, in a sense, the Father was "crucified with Christ, for Christ was one with the Father" (*Signs of the Times*, March 26, 1894). Yet, it was Christ who actually died in human form and paid the price on Calvary's cross. "Worthy is the Lamb that was slain" (Rev. 5:12). Only Christ was "the Lamb slain from the foundation of the world" (Rev. 13:8). No one but the slain Lamb was worthy to open the seven seals of the book, an illustration of Christ's unique and incomparable role. "And they sung a new song, saying, Thou art worthy to take the book, and to open the seals thereof: for thou wast slain, and hast redeemed us to God by thy blood" (Rev. 5:9).

It was not the Father but Christ who was slain, and it was Christ's blood that was shed to redeem fallen humanity.

---

38. "*All things Christ received from God*, but He took to give. So *in the heavenly courts*, in His ministry for all created beings: *through the beloved Son, the Father's life flows out to all*; through the Son it returns, in praise and joyous service, a tide of love, to *the great Source of all*" (*The Desire of Ages*, p. 21, emphasis supplied). Christ received all things from God His Father, the great Source of all things. Thus, He receives His Father's life and gives it to all creation. As the wisdom of God and the power of God (1 Cor. 1:24), the Son receives his Father's wisdom and gives it to His children when they ask (James 1:5); the Son receives His Father's power and gives it to those who receive Him as the Son of God that they may become sons of God (John 1:12). As the brightness of His Father's glory and the express image of His Father's person, the Son upholds all things by the word of his Father's power (Heb. 1:3).

Ellen White described God the Father, the Sovereign of the universe, investing His Son "with authority" that "devolved on Christ alone" (*Spirit of Prophecy*, vol. 1, p. 17; cf. *Patriarchs and Prophets*, p. 36): "The Father then made known that it was ordained by Himself that Christ should be equal with Himself" (*Signs of the Times*, Jan. 9, 1879).

Thus, Jesus Christ stands out in a unique and incomparable way in God's plan of salvation. Christ alone overcame our fallen humanity and took dominion of this world. For this reason, He was set at the "right hand in the heavenly places, far above all principality, and power, and might, and dominion, and every name that is named, not only in this world, but also in that which is to come" (Eph. 1:20, 21). Christ "humbled himself, and became obedient unto death, even the death of the cross. Wherefore God also hath highly exalted him, and given him a name which is above every name" (Phil. 2:8, 9).

The passage in 1 Corinthians 15:24–28 refers to the climax of the plan of salvation, when Christ's unique role as the sole Redeemer emerges into a glorious and total victory over sin and death, and over Satan and his false dominion. Christ stands out in the entire universe as the great Conqueror and as the lawful owner of this, once lost, planet earth. Christ, through His unique and incomparable, redeeming role, received a great honor above the Father—the privilege of being the legitimate owner and ruler of this world.

However, at the glorious end of the plan of salvation, Christ will step down from His outstanding, unique position and role, and subject Himself to the Father in the sense of restoring perfect equality between Himself and His Father as it existed before the foundation of the world (John 17:24). Says Paul, in 1 Corinthians 15: 28, "And when all things shall be subdued unto him, then shall the Son also himself be subject unto him that put all things under him, that God may be all in all"—in other words, that the Godhead may reign supreme as a whole, without Christ standing above the others, touting His own achievements.

Thus, Christ will ultimately share the legal privileges He has gained, exercising power and authority over this world with the Father. We find the fulfillment of this in Revelation 11:15, where we read: "The kingdoms of this world are become the kingdoms of our Lord, and of his Christ …" Thus, our Lord—the Father—will share with Christ equal rights and possession of the kingdoms of this world, lawfully obtained by the death of Christ on Calvary's cross.

Said Paul, in 1 Corinthians 15:24: "Then cometh the end, when he shall have delivered up the kingdom to God, even the Father; when he shall have put down all rule and all authority and power." Thus, at the end when Christ has victoriously and completely put to naught all forms of hostile powers, he will deliver up to His Father the kingdom of this world He has obtained and share the rights He has gained with Him. Equality between the Godhead will be restored.

Chapter 7

CHRIST, THE SOURCE OF WISDOM

The book of Proverbs belongs to the poetical books. In chapter 8 we find wisdom pictured as a crying woman putting forth her voice. Further on in this chapter, we find several allusions to the Son of God, and we clearly see wisdom personified in Christ, as depicting His nature and work.

In this chapter, we find a few texts that are rather problematic to some people. Although they understand that poetical expressions and descriptions cannot always be taken literally, yet they have a hard time getting around the fact that Christ is repeatedly pictured in this chapter as having been created or having been born before the foundation of the world.

Here are some expressions taken from the *New English Bible*, which clearly seem to indicate this:

> "The Lord created me the beginning of his works, before all else that he made, long ago. Alone, I was fashioned in times long past, at the beginning, long before earth itself . When there was yet no

ocean I was born, no springs brimming with water. Before the mountains were settled in their place, long before the hills I was born, when as yet he had made neither land nor lake, nor the first clod of earth. When he set the heavens in their place I was there, when he girdled the ocean with the horizon, when he fixed the canopy of clouds overhead and set the springs of ocean firm in their place ..." (Prov. 8:22–28).[39]

In this passage we notice clearly that Jesus Christ, as the Son of God and the personification of Wisdom, is pictured in relation to God's work of Creation. In the first chapter of the Bible, we read that God's creation was good and that on the sixth day: "God saw every thing that He had made, and, behold it was very good" (Gen. 1:31). Wisdom was not lacking at the Creation. The glorious work of Creation was a unique masterpiece of Wisdom.

Right after the Creation story, however, we read about the fall of man in sin. At that moment, there was with man no Wisdom anymore. Humanity had become foolish. We were then severely lacking in Wisdom, and God had provided a remedy. Proverbs 8 describes that Christ, before the work of Creation, was brought forth as the personification of wisdom. This wisdom-role of Christ towards fallen humanity was beforehand agreed upon.

Proverbs is a poetical book. Therefore, we need not be surprised to find it using rather poetical expressions. Thus, we can understand that we read in this chapter that Christ

---

39. See chapter 1 on the King James rendering of this passage.

was born. He was not born as a divine being. He was born in the role of wisdom.

My brother is a medical doctor. I do not remember the exact date *when* he received his medical degree or doctorate, but I still remember *that* he received it. Let us say it was on August 20, 1968. Now, suppose I would be inspired by a poetical spirit and would say, *My brother was born a physician on August 20, 1968*, would that mean then that he did not exist before that date? No, certainly not. He existed as a man some twenty-five years *before* that date, but *since* that date, he has existed in the role of a medical doctor.

Therefore, Christ was "born" in His wisdom-role before the Creation took place.[40] This does not mean that He was not in existence before that event. No, His existence as a divine being is from all eternity. Nonetheless, before the Creation, He was "born" into the role of wisdom, on behalf of man, should he succumb to sin.

Christ is the only Mediator between God and fallen man. We are "in Christ Jesus, who of God is made unto us wisdom" as well as "righteousness, and sanctification and redemption" (1 Cor. 1:30). It is interesting to note that for the word "made," the Greek word *ginomai* is used, which means "to be born or to be begotten." Thus, as described in Proverbs 8, it is clear that Christ was born in His wis-

---

40. Regarding Jesus' wisdom-role, Ellen White wrote: "Every sentence he uttered came from God. He was the Word and the Wisdom of God, and he ever presented truth with the authority of God" (*Special Testimonies on Education*, p. 6, written March 26, 1896). "But unto them which are called, both Jews and Greeks, Christ the power of God, and *the wisdom of God*" (1 Cor. 1:24, emphasis supplied).

dom-role on behalf of fallen humanity, which had become foolish by listening to the great deceiver.

As we read further, we see how Christ's wisdom-role is poetically pictured as a source of great delight:

> Then I was at his side each day, his darling and delight, playing in his presence continually, playing on the earth, when he had finished it, while my delight was in mankind. (Prov. 8:30, 31).

At the Creation, Christ was present as the personification of Wisdom. When the need should arise, He was ready to fulfill His newly adopted role. It is in this light that Christ is poetically described as being a "darling and delight," playing on the earth and finding delight in mankind. The Creation would not have been made in vain. A way of escape was secured. It is the way of wisdom, the way of righteousness, sanctification, and redemption. God's wonderful work of creation would not fail. His plan for this earth would surely succeed. This was a source of rejoicing. God said to Job: "Where wast thou when I laid the foundations of the earth? ... When the morning stars sang together, and all the sons of God shouted for joy?" (Job 38:4, 7).

Proverbs 8 does not offer support for the supposition that Christ was actually born as a divinely created being. David's statement in Psalms 2:7, "... the Lord hath said unto me, Thou art my Son; this day have I begotten thee," refers to Christ's resurrection from the dead. Paul connects Jesus' being "begotten" with the passage about His resurrection: "God hath fulfilled the same unto us their children, in that he hath raised up Jesus again; as it is also

Christ, the Source of Wisdom

written in the second psalm, Thou art my Son, this day have I begotten thee" (Acts 13:33). Paul also connects the declaration of Jesus as the Son of God with His being resurrected from the dead: "And declared to be the Son of God with power, according to the spirit of holiness, by the resurrection from the dead" (Rom. 1:4).

Thus, in full harmony with the Bible, Ellen White testified that there was never a time when Christ was not in close fellowship with the eternal God. He existed always as a divine being, even as the eternal Son of God, in union and oneness with His Father.

In answer to the questions posed at the beginning of this book, we conclude that Mrs. White did not go along with mistaken notions of the early pioneers in the name of unity, but corrected their mistaken concepts by describing the nature of God in detail over the years.[41] Even so, her early writings never contradicted the true biblical doctrine of the Trinity. Her repeated appeals to the original platform of eternal truth have to do with the acceptance of the real personality—the real personhood—of the Father and the Son.

---

41. Some of these amplifications are similar and comparable with the description of other authors such as Heman Humphrey, John Cumming, John Harris, and Henry Melvill. Thus, in God's providence, it is made clear that we, as a church, share our biblical concept of the Trinity with other Christians, which may help to inspire confidence that we are not a sectarian movement but a Christian church.

BIBLIOGRAPHY

Boardman, William E. *The Higher Christian Life.* Boston: Henry Hoyt, 1859.

The Book of Discipline of the United Methodist Church. Nashville: United Methodist Publishing House, 1988.

Cumming, John. *Sabbath Evening Readings. St. John.* Boston: John P. Jewett and Company, 1856.

Harris, John. *The Great Teacher: Characteristics of our Lord's Ministry,* with an introductory essay by Heman Humphrey. Amherst: J. S. and C. Adams, 1836.

Melvill, Henry. *Sermons by Henry Melvill.* 3rd ed., enlarged. Edited by C. P. McIlvaine. New York: Stanford and Swords, 1853, 1844.

Allen, Joseph Henry. *Ten Discourses on Orthodoxy.* Boston: American Unitarian Association, 1889.

Philip, John. *Rays of Light: or, Church-Themes and Life-Problems.* 8 vols. Edinburgh: Johnstone, Hunter, and Company, 1871.

Holt, Russel. "The Doctrine of the Trinity in the Seventh-day Adventist Denomination: Its Rejection and Acceptance." Term paper for Dr. Mervyn Maxwell, Seventh-day Adventists Theological Seminary, 1969.

Limborch, Philippus van. *The History of the Inquisition.* Translated by Samuel Chandler. 2 vols. London: J. Gray, 1731.

Trench, Richard Chenevix. *Synonyms of the New Testament.* London: Kegan Paul, Trench, Trübner, Company, Ltd, 1894.

Vincent, Marvin R. *Word Studies in the New Testament.* 4 vols. New York: Charles Scribner's Sons, 1889.

Waggoner, Ellet J. *Christ and His Righteousness.* Oakland, CA: Pacific Press Publishing Company, 1890.

White, Ellen G. *The Acts of the Apostles: In the Proclamation of the Gospel of Jesus Christ.* Mountain View, CA: Pacific Press Publishing Association, 1911.

———. *Christ's Object Lessons.* Washington, DC: Review and Herald Publishing Association, 1900, 1941.

———. *Christ Triumphant.* Hagerstown, MD: Review and Herald Publishing Association, 1999.

———. *Counsels on Health.* Mountain View, CA: Pacific Press Publishing Association, 1923, 1957.

———. *Early Writings of Ellen G. White.* Washington, DC: Review and Herald Publishing Association, 1882, 1945.

———. *The Desire of Ages: The Conflict of the Ages Illustrated in the Life of Christ.* Mountain View, CA: Pacific Press Publishing Association, 1898, 1940.

———. *The Great Controversy Between Christ and Satan: The Conflict of the Ages in the Christian Dispensation.* Oakland, CA: Pacific Press Publishing Association, 1888.

———. *The Great Controversy Between Christ and Satan: The Conflict of the Ages in the Christian Dispensation.* Mountain View, CA: Pacific Press Publishing Association, 1911.

———. *Manuscript Releases.* 21 vols. Silver Spring, MD, E. G. White Estate, 1981, 1987, 1990, 1993.

———. *The Ministry of Healing.* Mountain View, CA: Pacific Press Publishing Association, 1905, 1942.

———. *Our High Calling.* Washington, DC: Review and Herald Publishing Association, 1961.

———. *Patriarchs and Prophets.* Washington, DC: Review and Herald Publishing Association, 1890, 1958.

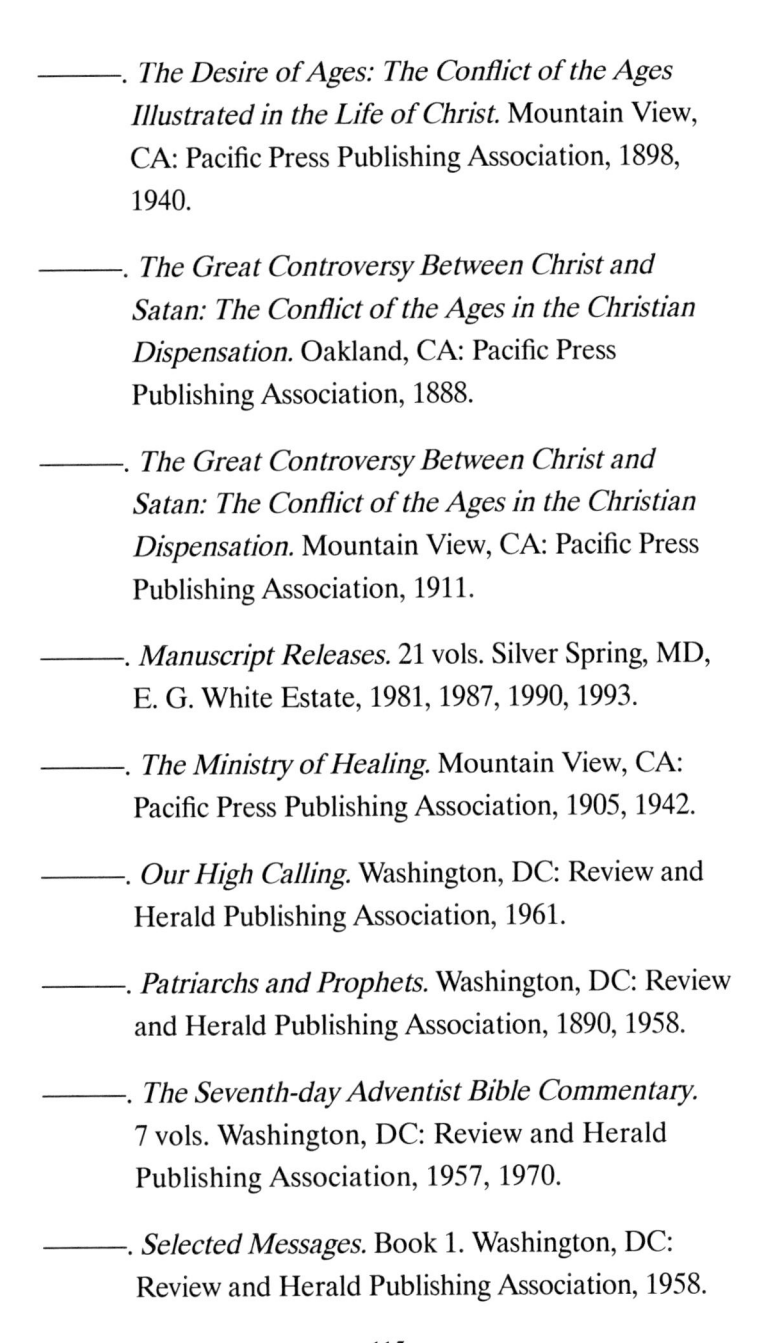

———. *The Seventh-day Adventist Bible Commentary.* 7 vols. Washington, DC: Review and Herald Publishing Association, 1957, 1970.

———. *Selected Messages.* Book 1. Washington, DC: Review and Herald Publishing Association, 1958.

―――. *Selected Messages.* Book 3. Washington, DC: Review and Herald Publishing Association, 1980.

―――. *Sermons and Talks.* 2 vols. Silver Spring, MD: Ellen G. White Estate, 1990, 1994.

―――. *A Sketch of the Christian Experience and Views of Ellen G. White.* Saratoga Springs, NY: James White, 1851.

―――. *Special Testimonies on Education.* No imprint, 1897.

―――. *Spirit of Prophecy.* Vol. 1. Battle Creek, MI: Steam Press of the SDA Publishing Association, 1870.

―――. *Spirit of Prophecy.* Vol. 4. Battle Creek, MI: Steam Press of the SDA Publishing Association,1884.

―――. *Spiritual Gifts.* Vol. 1. Battle Creek, MI: James White Publisher, 1858.

―――. *Spiritual Gifts.* Vol. 2. Battle Creek, MI: James White Publisher, 1860.

―――. *Spiritual Gifts.* Vol. 3. Battle Creek, MI: James White Publisher, 1864.

―――. *Spiritual Gifts.* Vol. 4. Battle Creek, MI: James White Publisher, 1864.

―――. *Steps to Christ.* Battle Creek, MI: Review and Herald Publishing Company, 1892.

———. *Supplement to the Christian Experience and Views of Ellen G. White.* Rochester, NY: James White, 1854.

———. *Testimonies for the Church.* Vol. 2. Mountain View, CA: Pacific Press Publishing Association, 1881, 1902, 1948 by the Ellen G. White Publications.

———. *Testimonies for the Church.* Vol. 8. Mountain View, CA: Pacific Press Publishing Association, 1904 by the Ellen G. White Publications.

———. *This Day With God.* Washington, DC: Review and Herald Publishing Association, 1979.

———. *Upward Look.* Washington, DC: Review and Herald Publishing Association, 1982.

Wilkinson, Benjamin George. *Truth Triumphant: The Church in the Wilderness.* Mountain View, CA: Pacific Press Publishing Association, 1944.

We invite you to view the complete
selection of titles we publish at:

www.TEACHServices.com

Scan with your mobile
device to go directly
to our website.

Please write or email us your praises, reactions, or
thoughts about this or any other book
we publish at:

TEACH Services, Inc.
P U B L I S H I N G
www.TEACHServices.com • (800) 367-1844

P.O. Box 954
Ringgold, GA 30736
info@TEACHServices.com

TEACH Services, Inc., titles may be purchased in bulk
for educational, business, fund-raising,
or sales promotional use.
For information, please e-mail:

BulkSales@TEACHServices.com

Finally, if you are interested in seeing
your own book in print, please contact us at

publishing@TEACHServices.com

We would be happy to review
your manuscript for free.